✠ ✠ ✠ ✠

THE Good Book Cookbook

NAOMI GOODMAN

ROBERT MARCUS

SUSAN WOOLHANDLER

Foreword by George M. Landes, D.D.

DODD, MEAD & COMPANY
NEW YORK

*The illustrations on pages 28, 54,
76, 98, 122, 144, 164, 188, and
202 are by Percival Goodman*

Copyright © 1986 by Naomi Goodman, Robert Marcus, and Susan Woolhandler

Published by Dodd, Mead & Company, Inc.
71 Fifth Avenue, New York, N.Y. 10003
Distributed in Canada by
McClelland and Stewart Limited, Toronto
Manufactured in the United States of America
Designed by Kay Lee

2 3 4 5 6 7 8 9 10

Library of Congress Cataloging-in-Publication Data

Goodman, Naomi.
  The Good Book cookbook.

  Bibliography: p.
  Includes index.
1. Cookery.   2. Food in the Bible.   I. Marcus, Robert,
1949–   II. Woolhandler, Susan.   III. Title.
IV. Title: Good Book cook book.
TX652.G66   1986   641.5   86-2096
ISBN 0-396-08578-4

CONTENTS

Foreword

While the Bible does not give primary attention to the foods people ate or to how they prepared them for consumption, beginning with God's gift to humanity of plants and fruit for food in Genesis 1, to a reference to the twelve kinds of fruit on the tree of life in Revelations 22, there is hardly a biblical chapter that does not contain some allusion to various types of food, or to cooking and eating. Unlike some of their Babylonian predecessors or later Roman successors, the biblical writers did not record any recipes for the meals they often mention in passing. Yet through a careful study of the ancient Near Eastern literary legacy, together with an investigation of how more recent Middle Eastern culinary experts have prepared the same foods our biblical ancestors ate, it is possible to visualize what a number of these meals were like.

And that is what the authors of this book have brilliantly done. With painstaking research and an informed imagination, they have provided an authentic quality to the fascinating array of recipes they present. Moreover, when readers try out such delectations as Rebekah's Savory Stew, or Queen Esther's Pomegranate Walnut Sauce, or portions from King Solomon's Feast menu, not only will they discover some exciting new taste experiences, but also find themselves in closer touch with an important aspect of life as it was lived in biblical times.

As one who has enjoyed a sampling of some of the fare contained within the following pages, I can attest to the gustatory delight in store for those who likewise would "satisfy [their] hearts with food and gladness" (Acts 14:17). Indeed for me, as I would hope also for others, it has added a fresh dimension to understanding the invitation of the ancient psalmist: "O taste and see that the Lord is good!" (Psalms 34:8).

George M. Landes, D.D.
Professor of Biblical Archaeology
Union Theological Seminary

Acknowledgments

We want to thank the many friends and colleagues who helped us to develop *The Good Book Cookbook* by sharing their expertise in different fields. Firstly, Dr. George Landes, Professor of Biblical Archaeology at Union Theological Seminary, our main consultant, who has been most generous with his time and knowledge. We would also like to express our gratitude to Rabbi Michael Robinson, Rev. Richard Baggett Deats, Pearl Braude, Margaret Beach, Woodford Beach, Belle Goldblum, Percival Goodman, Rachel Goodwoman, Andre Lubart, Constance Prescod, Mary Marcus, Renee Marton, Victoria Marcus Martin, Paola Nivola-Silvas, Daniel Schley, Suzanne Sutin, Barbara, Stephanie, and Anne Woolhandler, and finally, the folks down at Wolff Computer and, especially, our editor, Cynthia Vartan. Other scholars and cooking experts were consulted, but the final responsibility is that of the authors.

Abraham prepares a meal for the angels (Genesis 18:2–20)

Introduction

In *The Good Book Cookbook,* we invite you to enter biblical life through the kitchen door where you will discover a nourishing and often surprisingly sophisticated cuisine based on the Bible's many references to cooking and eating, generally amid settings of great rejoicing in the gift of food from God. Much of our information comes from these scriptural passages. We have developed recipes for specific dishes in the Bible, such as Esau's Pottage, Ezekiel's Bread, Roast Suckling Lamb, Fatted Calf, and Barley Cakes. Consulting biblical scholars and culinary experts, we have developed modern recipes for the meals eaten during this time, including royal feasts. We provide traditional foods for the religious festivals of the Hebrew Scriptures and the communal meals and holidays of the early Christians.

Our dishes are based on research into archaeological sources, biblical commentaries, classical writings, and the history of agriculture and food in the Middle East and Mediterranean areas. But as this book is a practical cookbook, recipes are listed under standard categories such as vegetables and desserts, not in historical sequence.

The cuisine of the Bible is naturally a healthful one. It embodies the principles recommended by nutritionists and physicians today. All bread and grain dishes were of whole grain and all milling was done with stones; hence there was important fiber in the diet. Vegetarian and dairy meals were popular. Beans, grains, and raw vegetables were eaten frequently, as were yogurt and simple cheeses. Poultry and fish were far more commonly served than meat, which was generally reserved for special occasions. Fruits and nuts were the main ingredients in fine sauces and desserts. Refined sugar did not exist and is not part of the recipes in this cookbook, but you will find other unusual sweeteners made from dates, grapes, and, of course, honey.

The site of the Holy Land—between the empires of the Fertile Crescent—made it a melting pot of culinary influences. And the extraordinary lives of many biblical men and women placed them in the royal courts of ancient civilizations throughout the Mediterranean and beyond.

The time frame represented in this book begins around 3000 B.C. at the campsites of the early pastoralists, who roasted choice meats at their firepits and baked bread on heated stones. It concludes around A.D. 100 at the communal suppers of the early Christians throughout the Roman Empire. Along the way, you will sample the bakeries of Pharoah's Egypt, the orchards of Babylonia, the spiceries of Persia, the health regimes of classical Greece, the elaborate banquets of imperial Rome, and the Last Supper of Jesus and his Disciples.

In the late Stone Age of Genesis, the families of Abraham, Isaac, and Jacob hunted wild birds, milked and managed their flocks, gathered the herbs that seasoned their foods, and tended their staple, still semiwild crops of barley, figs, and grapes. Savory stews, roasted lamb, grilled quail, fresh curd cheeses, macerated fruits, unleavened breads, and parched-grain salads are examples of the fresh "primitive" cuisine you will find in *The Good Book Cookbook.*

Advances in the kitchen arts came in Pharaoh's Egypt, along a fertile river valley famous for its abundant foodstuffs. The stonework of the Egyptian tombs has left us pictures of the kitchens, bakeries, gardens, and fisheries of the second millenium before Christ. (Some carvings remain so detailed that poultry can still be identified from the markings on its wings.) Here in Egypt the arts of baking and brewing blossomed. Actual pieces of petrified bread discovered in recent times testify to the use of leavenings. The records of the Pharaoh Ramses III list over a million loaves of various breads presented to their deity, Amon-Ra, probably eaten by the slaves who built the pyramids. We tell you how to recreate the naturally leavened breads, some topped with onions, stuffed with figs, or flavored with exotic spices from the Eastern caravans. A menu plan and recipes will enable you to prepare a sumptuous Egyptian-style banquet such as Moses would have known, distinguished by a variety of ducks, geese, and other marsh-loving fish and fowl. Our vegetable chapter suggests ancient ways to savor the succulent melons, pungent leeks, crisp radishes, and unusual lotus root dishes of ancient Egypt that caused the Hebrews to sigh with nostalgia in the Sinai desert after the Exodus (Numbers 11:5).

In the Promised Land, filled with milk and honey, wheat, grapes, barley, figs, and olives, the people of the Bible built a powerful nation-state founded on their unique religious principles. The principles, extending to the combining and handling of food, forbade the consumption of meat and dairy products in the same meal, thus distinguishing the cuisine of the Hebrews from all other Middle Eastern groups (although otherwise many of the same ingredients were used).

Our main objective is to gain insight into the daily lives of the people of the Bible through their unique methods of food preparation. We have tried to illustrate the differences in the cooking styles in the ancient Holy Land and the special relationship the Hebrews had with their animals, a relationship that governed the way meat and dairy dishes were prepared. We have, for instance, given examples of all the ways meat was prepared at the time, and you will find a number of unusual meat dishes, prepared with the wine, fruits, nuts, and herbs so abundant in the Holy Land. You will find a wealth of fresh fruit and herb salads, vegetable casseroles, and hearty bean and grain stews. We present delightful calcium-rich dairy dishes and give simple directions for making your own yogurts and curd cheeses to serve with homemade biblical breads. You can choose from a variety of traditional seasoning agents and condiments of the Holy Land, such as black onion seed, cumin, coriander, anise, cinnamon, cassia, must, grape honey, date syrup, rose water, orange flower water, capers, and ground pomegranate seed.

When the Israelites were conquered by Mesopotamia, Persia, Greece, and Rome, new foods and cooking styles were introduced. These empires have left literate recipes and cooking records, which, generally concerned with the splendor of the royal tables, were often more explicit and detailed than those in the Bible.

The oldest known "cookbook" is a set of Mesopotamian clay tablets, originally thought to be a pharmaceutical manual. As in all ancient cooking records so far discovered, there were no exact measurements given. And though the clay tablets of Mesopotamian cuneiform survived in greater number than the more fragile Egyptian papyri, the proper names of plants, spices, and condiments have been most difficult to decipher. Fortunately, a good translation exists of a list of produce from the gardens of the Babylonian King Merodach-Baladan, who is mentioned in Isaiah 39:1.

The tolerant Persians were next to take over the Holy Land and its people. Consummate traders and seamen, with an empire that stretched almost to India, the Persians introduced new plants, animals, and spices to their subjects and perfected a cuisine of legendary delicacy and abundance. The Book of Esther begins with a Persian banquet which lasted for one hundred and eighty days (Esther 1:1–6). Our selection of classical Persian foods will give you a taste of the enduring culinary legacy of this empire.

As the people of the Holy Land became part of the Greek and Roman empires, their dining and cooking styles expanded. The classical records on botany, dietary customs, and food technology are quite extensive, and include the cookbooks of Apicius, *De Re Coquinaria,* believed to have been written around the time of the early Christian church.

The imperial Romans were fond of large and sumptuous meals, and were forced to pass laws restricting extravagant feasts. Inspectors even attended banquets to keep the menu selections within established boundaries. So, too, the temperate early Christians needed a reminder from Paul that dignified appetite was the standard for the communal meals of the church (Jude 12). You may also need a reminder of restraint when you sample some of the treats of these ancient repasts through the recipes and menu plans of *The Good Book Cookbook.*

All our recipes serve six unless otherwise noted. Some of the ingredients may seem unfamiliar and exotic, but most of our recipes can be made easily, thanks to modern technology. Never have we appreciated our everyday kitchen appliances so much as when we mulled over the long hours the biblical homemakers spent parching, grinding, salting, drying, pickling, and otherwise preserving their harvest. Biblical cooks made everything from scratch, including the pots and pans.

Through this book we have tried to show you the seasonal rhythms of agriculture and the methods of food preservation that dominated ancient life in the Holy Land. To understand these methods is to understand the lifestyle of the Bible's people and eat a variety of satisfying meals at the same time.

We hope *The Good Book Cookbook* will bring to life some of the events recorded so eloquently in the Scriptures, many of which are noted in our recipes. Our biblical references to the harvesting, preserving, cooking, and consuming of food in everyday life are from the New King James Version (Thomas Nelson Publishers). We hope that you will enjoy preparing and consuming biblical meals as much as we have enjoyed developing, testing, and eating them.

MEAT

✠   ✠   ✠   ✠

Meat was a favorite food of the early Hebrew pastoralists, and the Bible frequently records its preparation as an homage to God. Throughout the first books of the Bible, appeals to God are sanctified by the ritual preparation of roasted animals. The results are often dramatic. After the great flood, God is moved to mercy for the evil of humanity by the sweet savor of Noah's burnt offerings (Genesis 8:21). The priesthood of Aaron is consecrated by Moses in the presentation of a fragrant barbecue (Leviticus 8:22–36). Thanksgiving was demonstrated and atonement for sins requested by the offering of grilled meat. Religious festivals, such as Passover, Easter, Pentecost, and Sukkoth called specifically for the roasting of whole animals. Offerings to God were always eaten, though certain parts of the animal were forbidden, such as the fat.

Hospitality and general rejoicing were also expressed through the roasting of fresh meat for guests, as in Abraham's feast for the angels of God (Genesis 18:2–8) and the preparation of the fatted calf (Luke 15:23). Lamb, goat, and beef were eaten.

The Hebrews were very strict about the handling of livestock, setting high standards for purity, cleanliness, and humane treatment. Animals were thought to have the same God-given flame of life as man. This life was in their blood, which could not be consumed. Animals were inspected for abnormalities by the priests and rejected if deemed unfit. Only animals of certain categories were fit for consumption. These laws were recorded in the Book of Leviticus and are known as kasruth or kosher. They remain the essence of an ancient systematic respect for life that distinguished the Hebrews and later the Christians from their pagan neighbors. The laws are still followed by many Jews.

These regulations tightened the bonds of community among the Hebrews and discouraged converts to the religion. The Hebrews could rarely socialize with their neighbors over ordinary meals or at the pagan banquets, which frequently featured the pork, camel, rabbit, and shrimp forbidden them. Most ancient societies had rules and traditions regarding the preparation of meat, but few were as strict and ritualized as the Hebrews'.

Many of the dietary laws, such as the systematic inspection of meat and the prohibition against eating scavenger animals, seem reasonable today. Others, such as the prohibition of camel meat, profoundly limited the living space and lifestyle of the Hebrews. Forbidden the flesh of camels, they could not easily rove the deserts that surrounded them.

By the time of Jesus, these "ancient" attitudes toward food were changing. Many Jews felt the Temple and later the synagogues were not the place for the processing of meat. Eventually these functions were housed separately and put under the jurisdiction of a professionaly trained religious authority called the *shochet*. The requirement that no unnecessary pain be inflicted upon the animal was still of utmost importance.

Jesus renounced the kosher restrictions for his followers in Mark 7:19 by declaring all food clean. And as new converts streamed into the church, the Disciples considered which food laws should be kept by those unversed in the ancient Hebrew creed. But the Jerusalem council continued to uphold certain strictures regarding blood and the handling of animals (Acts 15:20). The ancient belief that blood implied life was enshrined in the Christian sacrament of communion.

Roasting and stewing meat with the local herbs and vegetables were the basic cooking methods of the Patriarchs. As the people of the Holy Land came into contact with the Persians, Greeks, and Romans, and new spices and plants became available, their cuisine became more varied and elaborate. In this section we recreate some meat dishes of antiquity, from biblical times through the Roman foods of early Christian times.

Veal With Almond Curd Sauce

The hospitality of Abraham to the angels of God is recorded in Genesis 18:2–20. This meal is the occasion of a gift from the Lord. Abraham and Sarah are to have a son, the child for which Sarah has longed, despite her advanced age. At this early juncture, the Hebrews had not received the law against consuming milk and meat together. Veal in a rich cream sauce is still a traditional feast dish of the Middle East, as it has been for millenniums.

$\frac{1}{4}$ cup freshly roasted
  almonds
1$\frac{1}{2}$ teaspoons each cumin
  seed and coriander seed
$\frac{1}{4}$ teaspoon salt
2 teaspoons ginger, finely
  shredded
1 or 2 cloves garlic
2 teaspoons honey
2 pounds veal scallops

2 tablespoons oil or butter
1 medium onion, sliced
1 tablespoon grated orange
  or lemon peel
2 cinnamon sticks
$\frac{1}{2}$ cup vermouth or light veal
  stock
1 cup light cream or whole
  milk yogurt

Grind almonds with cumin, coriander, salt, ginger, garlic, and honey in a blender, food processor, or mortar and pestle to form a paste. (If using a blender, add a few tablespoons of the vermouth or stock to facilitate blending.) In a large heavy skillet, brown veal scallops in oil or butter. Set aside. Brown onion in the same oil or butter. Add almond spice paste to browned onions and gently fry. Add water to keep from burning. Add grated peel, cinnamon sticks, and stock or wine and simmer for 10 minutes. Return veal to skillet and continue to simmer on low heat, about 15 minutes or until veal is cooked through. Add cream or yogurt and heat thoroughly. Do not allow to boil, as this will give an undesirable curdled texture to the sauce. Keep sauce at a simmer. Serve with hot Whole Wheat Sourdough Bread, Basic Barley, and a salad. Serve Sweet Millet Balls for dessert.

Rebekah's Savory Stew

So Rebekah spoke to Jacob her son, saying, "Indeed I heard your father speak to Esau your brother saying, 'Bring me game and make savory food for me that I may eat it and bless you in the presence of the Lord before my death.' Now therefore my son, obey my voice according to what I command you. Go to the flock and bring me from there two choice kids of the goats and I will make savory food from them for your father, such as he loves." Genesis 27:6–9

Stewing was the popular method of cooking fresh meat, and the matriarchs knew how to make domestic meat taste as rich as game. Here is a selection of stews using ingredients that were available.

Lamb Stewed With Figs and Wine

3 pounds boneless lamb,
  goat, or venison, cubed
2 tablespoons olive oil
2 or 3 cloves garlic
1½ cups red wine
½ cup water

2 teaspoons dry mustard
2 teaspoons ground coriander
2 teaspoons ground cumin
1 cup dried figs, halved
Salt to taste

Trim the meat of fat. In a stew pot, brown the cubed meat in olive oil. Mash the garlic and add to the browning meat for the last 2 or 3 minutes of cooking. Add the wine, water, mustard, spices, and figs. Bring to a boil. Cover and simmer for 90 minutes. Goat as well as large cubes of lamb will require 2 hours to cook. Salt to taste and serve with Basic Barley, Basic Millet, or bulghar wheat, a watercress salad, and Raisin Cake.

Savory Stew With Quinces and Pears

Quinces were a popular fruit of antiquity, cooked in sauces much as we use the tomato. Wild pears, not yet as sweet as our modern fruits, were also eaten. Combine these fruits or double the quantity of one for an unusual savory stew.

3 pounds lamb, beef, or
  veal, cubed
1 medium onion, sliced
2 tablespoons oil or butter
½ teaspoon ground ginger or
  2 teaspoons fresh ginger,
  grated
¼ teaspoon cinnamon

½ cup parsley, chopped
2 cups lamb or beef stock
  (bouillon cubes in water
  may be used as a last
  resort)
3 quinces, cored and sliced
3 pears, cored and sliced
Salt and pepper to taste

In a stewing pot with cover, sauté the meat and onion in oil or butter with the ginger and cinnamon until browned and fragrant. Add the chopped parsley and sauté for one minute. Add the stock, cover, and simmer for 40 minutes. Chop the quinces and pears into cubes and add to the pot. Cover and simmer for 40 minutes to an hour. Salt and pepper to taste. Serve with Basic Barley or Basic Millet, Marinated Lotus Root Salad, and Honey Fried Nuts.

Savory Stew With Lentils and Raisins

The ancient casserole dish was known as an *ilpas*. It was broad and shallow with a tight-fitting lid that had a hole for the escape of steam and the pouring off of extra liquid.

2 pounds lamb, beef, or veal, cubed
2 tablespoons oil
1 medium onion, sliced
½ teaspoon ground ginger
¼ teaspoon ground cinnamon
1 teaspoon ground cumin
3 cups lamb or beef stock (bouillon cubes may be used)

1 cup lentils
½ pound raisins, soaked overnight in ½ cup wine or water
Salt and pepper to taste
2 tablespoons honey (optional)
1 teaspoon orange flower water (optional)

In a stewing pot with cover, brown meat cubes in oil. Add onion and stir as onion browns. Add spices and stock. Cook for 5 minutes. Add lentils, cover, and cook for one hour. Add raisins and continue simmering, covered, for 20 minutes. Add salt and pepper. Add honey if a sweeter taste is desired. Stir orange flower water into the stew just before serving. Serve with Basic Barley, Onion, Olive, and Orange Salad, and Fig Cake.

Pomegranate Walnut Lamb (See Pomegranate Walnut Duck, page 44.)

Lamb Shish Kebabs With Roast Barley and Vegetables

The consumption of lamb was surrounded by spiritual significance for many peoples of the Fertile Crescent. The Hebrews considered lamb a great delicacy. The Egyptians valued the milk and wool so highly that taboos developed prohibiting regular consumption of the meat.

2 pounds lamb chunks, trimmed and suitable for kebabs

MARINADE

1 cup red wine
½ cup olive oil
1 clove garlic
3 or 4 juniper berries

2 bay leaves
½ cup apricot nectar
Pinch of cinnamon
Salt to taste

ROAST BARLEY

Prepare 2 cups barley by toasting on a cookie sheet or flat pan in the oven at 350°F until lightly browned. Place barley in saucepan with 2½ cups water and one tablespoon olive oil. Bring to a boil, then turn down heat, cover, and simmer until barley is tender, about 40 minutes. To make barley fluffy, place a dish towel or paper towel between pan and lid after cooking. Let sit 5 minutes.

HOLY LAND VEGETABLES FOR SHISH KEBABS

Parboiled pearl onions

Chunks of white turnip, parboiled or raw

Artichoke hearts

Broccoli flowerets

Radishes

Chunks of parboiled par-
snips

Parboiled lotus root, in chunks, or water chestnuts

TO PREPARE SHISH KEBABS

Marinate lamb chunks for at least one hour. Drain, reserving marinade. Place vegetables in marinade for a few minutes, then drain, reserving marinade again. On top of stove,
bring marinade to a boil, reduce heat, and simmer. Thread
lamb chunks and vegetables on skewers. Grill over a charcoal
fire, or broil at 375°F, about 10 to 15 minutes, basting with
marinade.

On serving platter, place roast barley and top with kebabs.
Pour marinade over all. Salt to taste. Serve with Rose Apple
Salad, Fava Bean or Lentil Salad, and Honey Cheesecake.

Stuffed Breast of Lamb With Raisin Sauce

Barley and lentils were the daily food of the working people
in ancient Israel. They are mentioned as provisions for David's army in 2 Samuel 17:28. Here they are combined with
an economical cut, breast of lamb (perfect for stuffing), and
topped with a rich, fruity sauce. Breast of veal can also be
used.

1 3- to 4-pound breast of lamb or veal, trimmed of excess fat

STUFFING

1½ cups cooked barley (see Basic Recipe, page 101)

1½ cups cooked lentils

1 tablespoon fresh or 1 teaspoon dried thyme leaves

1 tablepoon fresh or 1 teaspoon dried mint leaves

1 tablespoon black cumin seed

1 teaspoon marjoram

Salt to taste

RAISIN SAUCE

1 cup raisins soaked overnight in brandy or grape juice to cover

½ cup apricot curd or jam (unsweetened if possible)

Vinegar or lemon to taste (more will be needed if grape juice is used instead of brandy)

Wash meat and pat dry. Combine stuffing ingredients, stuff lamb or veal breast, and secure with string. Place on rack in oven preheated to 400°F for 10 minutes. Turn down temperature and slow roast at 350°F for about 20 minutes per pound. Meanwhile, combine the raisin sauce ingredients and heat gently, adding a little water to thin if desired. During the last 5 minutes of cooking, spoon some of the raisin sauce onto meat and increase heat to let sauce glaze the meat. Serve additional raisin sauce alongside. Accompaniments could include a selection of tart pickles, olives, and Arugola Rose Salad. Serve Cinnamon Cheese with Whole Wheat Pitas for dessert.

Rack of Lamb With Must Sauce

A rack of lamb is as impressive a centerpiece to a feast today as it was in the time of King Solomon. This roast is garnished with must, mustard seeds mashed into grape jelly, an ancient condiment.

2 racks of lamb (about 2 $\frac{1}{2}$ cup olive oil
   pounds each)   Salt to taste

Racks of lamb should be purchased from a butcher who can crack and french the bones. The bones will need to be covered with parchment or foil during cooking. Preheat oven to 400°F. Brush racks with olive oil. Place in a roasting pan, meaty side up, and roast approximately 25 minutes. Brush with must sauce and roast an additional 10 minutes. If you are using a meat thermometer, it should read 145°F for rare. Salt to taste. Serve with Millet Pilav, Figs in Red Wine and Cream, and Pistachio Almond Cookies.

MUST SAUCE
$\frac{1}{3}$ cup whole-grain mustard   Fresh grapes (optional)
$\frac{2}{3}$ cup grape honey, jelly, or
   jam

In a saucepan combine mustard and grape honey or jelly, adjusting for taste. Add fresh grapes and heat, stirring frequently until warmed through.

Leg of Lamb With Cumin, Mustard, and Pulse (Beans)

Cumin and mustard, two of the most popular Holy Land spices, combine deliciously to flavor the lamb and beans.

1 cup pea beans
½ cup chickpeas
3 cups water
½ cup lentils
1 leg of lamb, trimmed of
   fat
2 teaspoons ground cumin
2 teaspoons dry mustard or
   3 tablespoons prepared

1 teaspoon salt
4 cloves garlic, minced
¼ cup olive oil
¼ cup wine or grape juice
2 tablespoons whole wheat
   flour

Soak beans and chickpeas overnight. Boil in same water for 1½ hours, adding the lentils after the first hour. While beans are cooking, combine cumin, mustard, salt, garlic, oil, wine or juice, and flour into paste. Rub the paste on the lamb and let sit for at least one hour. Preheat oven to 350°F. Place lamb in a roasting pan on a rack and roast for one hour. Turn off oven. Add the partially cooked beans to the roasting pan, stirring the juices into the beans. Let rest in the warmed oven for one half hour. Turn on heat to 350°F and cook one half hour more for a five-pound leg. Add 15 minutes cooking time for each pound above five. Serve with Sumerian Watercress, Baked Celery and Fennel, and Pistachio Almond Cookies.

Grilled Lamb Kidneys

Kidneys were special delicacies in biblical times. They were associated with the peace offerings of Leviticus 3:4.

12 lamb kidneys

$\frac{3}{4}$ cup olive oil

$\frac{3}{4}$ cup white wine

2 tablespoons each oregano, parsley, and coriander

2 teaspoons thyme

2 cloves garlic, minced

Splash of vinegar

Touch of honey

Process kidneys by removing skin and white cores. Cut kidneys in half. Marinate in the oil, wine, herbs and spices, vinegar, and honey for at least a half hour, turning frequently. Choose grilling method: skewers over charcoal are a tasty favorite, but grilling under a hot broiler has the advantage of allowing the pan drippings to be caught. Grill the cut side first. Five minutes on each side is generally sufficient. Do not overcook; kidneys should be slightly pink at the center. Serve with Basic Bulghar, Grilled Leeks and Scallions, and Honey Cake. Veal kidneys may be cooked and served the same way.

Crown Roast of Lamb With Pomegranate Raisin Sauce

. . . I have roasted meat and eaten it . . .   Isaiah 44:19

1 6- to 8-pound crown roast of lamb (have butcher french the bones, i.e., scrape the bones clean from the end of the chop to the eye of the meat)

4 cloves garlic, mashed

½ cup fresh pomegranate juice (substitute tart grape juice or apple cider if necessary)

3 cups Basic Barley or Cracked Wheat Pilav (see pages 101 and 106)

POMEGRANATE RAISIN SAUCE

2 tablespoons almond oil

2 tablespoons whole wheat pastry flour

1½ cups pomegranate juice (substitute grape juice or apple cider if necessary)

½ cup seedless raisins

1 teaspoon orange rind, grated

1 tablespoon brandy

1 teaspoon prepared mustard

Salt to taste

To prepare sauce: Combine oil and flour in a saucepan into a smooth paste. Add fruit juice and raisins. Bring to a boil, stirring constantly. Simmer for 10 minutes. Add remaining ingredients and simmer an additional 20 minutes minimum.

To prepare the crown roast: Rub cleaned surfaces with cut garlic and fresh pomegranate juice if available. Cover the bones with aluminum foil. Place into an oven preheated to 450°F. Immediately turn the temperature down to 325°F and roast 17 to 30 minutes per pound—17 minutes for rare, 30 for well done. (A meat thermometer may be used; 145°F indicates rare.)

Forty minutes before the roast is finished, remove from oven and fill center with cooked barley or bulghar (cracked wheat). Glaze roast with pomegranate raisin sauce 10 minutes before cooking is finished and serve additional warm sauce at table. Serve with a Goat Cheese and Spinach Souffle, Homemade Olives, Fresh Fig and Grape Salad, and Honey Wine Cake.

Ground Meat With Bulghar (Lamb Kibbeh)

Thus shall they prepare the lamb, the grain offering and the oil . . .   Ezekiel 46:15

Kibbeh has been the "hamburger" of the Holy Land for millenniums. The whole-grain bulghar not only extends the meat, but also adds fiber and crunchy texture.

2 cups bulghar wheat
5 cups boiling water
1 pound ground lamb
 (ground beef may be
 used)

2 teaspoons cumin
1 onion, minced
Salt and pepper to taste
Oil for frying

Soak the bulghar in the boiling water. Let sit for about 30 minutes or until water is absorbed. Squeeze out excess water with hands or a towel. Mix with lamb, cumin, onion, salt, and pepper.

To bake: Spread mixture on a shallow, oiled baking pan and score the top with a knife diagonally to make diamond-shaped portions. Bake in a moderate oven (350°F) for about 25 minutes or until a knife inserted into meat comes out clean. Place under broiler to brown the top.

To fry: Form patties, like hamburgers, or into oblongs like thick fingers. Put in refrigerator for about an hour. Fry in hot oil, turning on all sides to form a good crust.

Serve with Whole Wheat Sourdough Bread, Yogurt and Sesame Sauce, Fava Bean Purée, lettuce, and radishes.

VEGETARIAN KIBBEH

In place of meat, substitute:

$\frac{1}{2}$ cup cooked lentils   2 eggs, beaten
$\frac{1}{4}$ cup olive oil

Proceed as above.

Roast Suckling Lamb

And Samuel took a suckling lamb and offered it as a whole burnt offering to the Lord.   1 Samuel 7:9–10

Throughout the Bible there are accounts of feasts inaugurated with preparation of a roast baby lamb or goat kid. Passover and Easter, the spring holidays, traditionally call for the serving of roasted lamb. In fact, lamb was so intimately associated with Easter that a lamb fashioned of pastry or sugar was often used simply as a centerpiece on the holiday table.

1 whole baby lamb (about 25 pounds, or one pound per person for adults)
4 heads garlic (about 30 cloves)
3 tablespoons salt
5 tablespoons ground coriander
5 tablespoons cumin
1 bunch fresh thyme
3 cups olive oil

Rotisserie cooking: Have the animal dressed for roasting. With mortar and pestle, crush the garlic, salt, and several sprigs of thyme and spices, and combine with olive oil. Rub all surfaces and cavities with the seasoned oil. Let lamb stand for at least 15 minutes. Push the spit of a large outdoor rotisserie unit through the lamb from breast to hindquarters. Tie the lamb's legs together. Suspend the lamb about three feet over a glowing charcoal fire and rotate every 10 to 15 minutes, basting with the seasoned oil. The lamb must be watched carefully. Have water close by to keep any flames in check.

Test the lamb after 2½ hours. Determine how your diners prefer their meat, since many people eat lamb quite rare. Depending on size, 3 to 3½ hours will be the maximum cooking time. The outside of the lamb should be crisp and golden. Transfer the lamb to a large serving tray.

Oven cooking: Place in oven preheated to 450°. Immediately turn temperature down to 350°. Oven roasting is best done on a rack with a meat thermometer. Internal temperature should be 160° to 165°F for rare, 175° to 180°F for well done. Serve the lamb with a selection of typical Holy Land relishes: grated radish, Must Sauce, brown cumin seeds, black cumin seeds, coriander leaves and toasted sesame seed, mint vinegar, and coarse salt.

The Fatted Calf (Goat or Lamb)

And bring the fatted calf here and kill it and let us eat and be merry.   Luke 15:23

The return of the prodigal son in the Gospel According to Luke was marked with the roasting of a whole young goat.

Sheep and goats were herded together in Bible times and called small cattle. Young goat, or chevon, is today becoming more available on commercial markets. The male of the species must be procured quite young, under four months, to ensure tenderness. The preparation of goat is similar to that of lamb, and there are many ways to cook a whole animal without a sophisticated rotisserie. For instance, one can improvise barbecue methods similar to those used centuries ago:

1. Dig a pit slightly wider and longer than the animal (10 to 12 inches deep for a small animal, 18 to 24 for a larger one). An auxiliary pit, connected by a trench to the main pit, is useful for starting and maintaining coals which can be easily moved into the main pit as more are needed.

2. Green branches can be laid across the fire pit to support the animal if substantial cutlery and muscle power is available to turn the roast (which will weigh twenty to forty pounds).

3. The best method is to spit the animal. (By the time of Jesus, homes of any means would have possessed iron stakes particularly designed for this purpose. A long iron spit would complete the equipment.) Two forked tree branches of relatively equal height, even whole young forked trees, can be used. Each branch must be inserted at least a foot into the ground for stability.

4. The spit itself is made more efficient if three holes are drilled into it at the approximate places where the hindquarters, middle, and shoulders of the animal will be. Perpendicular skewers can then be inserted through the holes and into the animal to hold it in place. A handle at the end of the spit is also very helpful.

5. The animal is spitted from the mouth to just below the tail. Wiring can be used to secure the animal.

6. Turn the spit regularly, steadily if possible. Brush the animal with olive oil as it cooks. Rosemary branches tied together make a good sop to brush olive oil on the lamb or goat. Season the olive oil with crushed garlic, onion, or shallots, and coriander, parsley, dill, oregano, celery seed, fennel seed, capers, crushed myrtle berries, cumin, and mint as desired.

7. A nice crust should form on the outside of the animal as a result of regular turning and oiling. For a superior crust, mix several tablespoons of honey with the final glazing of olive oil. The heated honey will caramelize, making a luscious brown crust. Date syrup can also be used.

8. Test for doneness by attempting to crack the thigh bone. If the bone moves easily, cooking is complete. Cooking time will be between 3 and 4 hours.

9. The roasting of a fatted calf is not a hurried affair. The fire should be started an hour or more before the cooking begins. Divide tasks so that people can cooperate and take part.

Have water handy to sprinkle on flame flare-ups. Serve with Fava Bean Purée, Lentil Salad, Onion, Olive, and Orange Salad, and Honey Cakes.

Saddle of Venison With Hot Apricot Sauce

King Solomon kept herds of deer, roebucks, and gazelle as domestic cattle. Hunting was not a routine manner of providing meat for the Hebrew table, as the animal had to be captured alive and humanely slaughtered according to the laws of Leviticus. 1 Kings 4:23 specifies that venison was prepared daily for the royal table.

1 cup beef suet or poultry fat (chicken, duck, or goose) or one cup olive oil

10 to 15 cloves garlic, slivered

1 6- to 7-pound saddle of young venison

Fresh or dried thyme, marjoram, and oregano

Preheat oven to 550°F. Melt fat in a saucepan, add garlic slivers, and stir to blend, browning slightly if a less pronounced garlic flavor is preferred. Make slits in the venison and insert the saturated garlic pieces. Rub entire roast with the remaining fat or oil. Sprinkle with herbs. Place in oven. Cook 10 minutes, then turn down heat to 350°F and cook 20 minutes per pound, basting frequently with fat and pan juices. Use the apricot sauce for the last basting, to glaze the meat. Turn up the heat for a time to achieve a crisp glaze. Serve additional sauce on the side.

Older venison needs to be marinated before cooking. Use equal parts olive oil and wine or tart grape juice with additional herbs. Venison is quite lean, so some kind of additional fat will be needed if the garlic in oil is not used. Strips of beef fat, or bacon or pork fat, can be inserted in place of garlic.

HOT APRICOT SAUCE

$1\frac{1}{2}$ cups sherry or sweet wine

$\frac{1}{4}$ teaspoon cumin

$\frac{1}{4}$ teaspoon coriander

1 teaspoon dry mustard

$\frac{1}{4}$ cup apricot nectar

1 tablespoon citrus rind, freshly grated

2 to 3 tablespoons vinegar (to taste)

½ cup raisins
½ cup slivered almonds
½ cup apricot preserves (unsweetened if possible)

1 tablespoon honey
(optional)
Salt to taste

Heat sherry or wine and add cumin, coriander, mustard, raisins, and almonds. Simmer 10 minutes, then add all other ingredients except salt. Balance the sweet and sour aspects of the sauce with additional vinegar or honey to your taste. Salt to taste.

Serve the venison with a pickled fish appetizer, Millet Pilav, Sumerian Watercress, Whole Baked Onions, fresh fruit, and Honey Wine Cake.

Roast Beef With Horseradish Walnut Sauce

The walnut was called the Persian nut in biblical times, in honor of its likely place of origin. The Persians and their emissaries, such as Nehemiah, were wealthy enough to eat meat every day (Nehemiah 5:18).

3 leeks, chopped, or one
bunch green onions,
chopped
1 tablespoon whole or
coarse grained mustard

2 bay leaves, crumbled
½ teaspoon thyme
2 tablespoons sweet red
wine or grape juice
1 3-pound roast beef

Mash leeks or onions, mustard, herbs, and wine or grape juice into a paste and rub over meat. Place on a rack and into an oven preheated to 400°F. Turn heat down to 350°F and roast 15 minutes per pound for rare, 17 for medium, 20 for well done. Prepare the Horseradish Walnut Sauce to serve alongside.

HORSERADISH WALNUT SAUCE

Though the kosher Hebrews had to forego cream sauces on meat, such sauces continued as favorites among other people of the biblical lands. This sauce is also delicious on hard-boiled eggs.

1 cup sour cream
½ cup plain yogurt
2 tablespoons fresh-grated
   horseradish (or prepared,
   if necessary)
1 teaspoon whole-grain
   mustard

1 teaspoon honey
1 tablespoon wine or juice
   (preferably that used on
   roast)
¼ cup coarsely chopped or
   ground walnuts

Combine all ingredients. May be served cold or at room temperature. As with all cream sauces, this one may be heated but will curdle if boiled, though curdling does not affect the taste. Serve with Arugola Rose Salad, Homemade Olives, and Raisin, Barley, and Apricot Pudding.

Roman Beef Sauté With Onions and Ginger

An ancient pot that could be used for sautéing was the *kedera*. It had a rounded bottom like a wok and two handles. The name means black in Hebrew, as the bottom was blackened from constant use.

½ cup onion rings, thinly
  sliced
1 tablespoon garlic, minced
1 tablespoon vegetable oil
2 pounds round steak, well
  trimmed and cut into
  bite-size cubes
1 cup mushrooms, sliced
2 tablespoons ginger,
  minced

1½ tablespoons Fish Sauce
  (see page 73)
½ tablespoon honey
1½ tablespoons red wine
  vinegar
½ cup scallions, chopped
2 tablespoons coriander
  leaves, chopped

Heat oil in a skillet and sauté onion rings until golden. Add garlic and continue to sauté briefly. Add beef cubes and mushrooms. Continue to sauté, stirring. Add ginger. In a small cup, mix Fish Sauce, honey, and vinegar. Add to skillet, stir, and cover. Simmer 4 to 5 minutes, adding a bit of water if necessary. Add scallions and coriander at the last moment. Stir. Serve with Basic Barley, Millet, or Bulghar.

Coriander Beef Roast With Roman Coriander Dipping Sauce

In Exodus 16:31, the taste of manna was likened to that of coriander seed, a plant indigenous to the Holy Land. The leaves, stalks, seeds, and roots of the coriander plant are edible. Coriander is also called cilantro or Chinese parsley.

3 cloves garlic, mashed
3 tablespoons prepared mustard
2 tablespoons ground coriander seed

2 tablespoons fresh coriander root, chopped (optional)
1 3- to 4-pound beef roast
5 stalks celery (optional)

Mash the garlic, mustard, and coriander seed and root into a paste with a mortar or blender. Rub the paste over the meat and let it sit at room temperature for an hour. Roast should be room temperature for cooking. Place on a roasting rack or improvise by laying five stalks of celery across the bottom of a roasting pan. Place the meat fat side up on the celery. Preheat oven to 400°F and roast meat for 10 minutes. Reduce heat to 350°F and cook 15 minutes per pound for rare, 17 for medium, and 20 for well done. Let meat rest for 10 minutes before slicing. Serve with Roman Coriander Dipping Sauce, barley pilav, and a compote of stewed fruits such as figs, dates, pears, and raisins. Honey-Fried Walnuts or Cinnamon Cheese is a nice dessert.

ROMAN CORIANDER DIPPING SAUCE

3 tablespoons Fish Sauce
   (see page 73)
2 tablespoons water
2 teaspoons vinegar

6 tablespoons fresh coriander leaves, chopped
2 scallions, chopped

Combine all ingredients. Let sit at least 10 minutes. This dipping sauce is excellent with all roasted or grilled meats and poultry, hot or cold.

Roman Ham With Sweet Herb Sauces

Smoked pork was a special favorite of the Romans, as lamb was of the Semitic people. Roman soldiers received standard rations of bacon, and smoked hams of domestic pork and wild boar graced the holiday tables. The recipes here are based on translations of Apicius, the Roman gourmet writer.

COOKING HAM

Uncooked ham should be baked about 20 minutes per pound at 350°F or until the internal temperature is 160°F. Precooked hams are baked to an internal temperature of 140°F, about 10 to 15 minutes per pound. To glaze the ham with a sauce, remove the ham from the oven about 30 minutes before it is done. Cut off most of the rind, leaving a ring around the shank bone. Make slashes across the fatty top side. Turn up oven to 400°F. Brush ham with sweet sauce or honey. Put ham back in oven and turn heat down to 300°F.

SWEET ANISE SAUCE

¾ teaspoon ground anise
  seed
¼ teaspoon cumin
1 teaspoon powdered mus-
  tard
⅓ cup fresh or dried dates,
  chopped

½ cup white wine
3 tablespoons honey
2 teaspoons vinegar
1 tablespoon olive oil
2 cups pork or chicken
  stock
Salt to taste

If possible, grind the anise seed, cumin seed, and mustard seed fresh. Mash dates and place all ingredients except salt in a saucepan. Bring to a boil, then simmer until liquid is reduced to 1½ cups. Put through blender if dates are not well incorporated into the sauce. Salt to taste and season with additional vinegar for tartness, honey for sweetness if desired. Glaze ham with anise seed sauce and/or serve alongside. This sauce is also good with cold ham. Serve with Barley Herb Soup, Candied Beet Preserve, Red Cabbage With Raisins, and Date Nut Bread.

ROSEMARY MINT SAUCE

2 tablespoons fresh or dried
  mint (less if dried),
  chopped
1 teaspoon rosemary
2 tablespoons chopped
  chives
½ teaspoon celery seed
¼ cup ground almonds

½ cup red wine
1 teaspoon vinegar
1 teaspoon honey
1 cup pork or chicken stock
2 tablespoons ham
  drippings
Salt to taste

Grind all spices fresh if possible; otherwise use ground. Put all ingredients except salt in a saucepan. Bring to a boil, then simmer until liquid is reduced by half. Salt to taste.

Ham Steaks With Figs

The Romans, like many ancient (and modern) people, were conscious of the effect an animal's diet had upon the flavor of its meat. Choice animals were fed on figs, carob pods, and parsnips to sweeten their flesh. In Luke 15:16, the prodigal son observes, ruefully, that the pigs eat better than he does.

6 ham steaks or thick slices
 of ham
3 tablespoons honey
2 to 3 tablespoons mild prepared mustard
2 cups fresh or canned figs, halved
Sprinkle of cinnamon
¼ cup vermouth, sweet
 white or red wine, juice
 of canned figs
Green grapes

Cut a small piece of fat off one of the ham slices and rub the bottom of an ovenproof dish to grease it. Mix the honey and mustard together and coat the ham steaks with the mixture. Arrange the steaks in the ovenproof dish, layering if necessary. Top with figs and sprinkle with cinnamon. Add vermouth, white or red wine, or juice from canned figs. Cover and bake in oven for 45 minutes at 325°F. Garnish with green grapes. Serve with Basic Barley, steamed cabbage, and a watercress salad.

POALTRY

✠   ✠   ✠   ✠

Poultry was a common food of the Holy Land. Jesus uses the abundance of small birds in the marketplace as a metaphor for God's watch over all creatures (Luke 12:6, Matthew 10:29), and the laws of Leviticus indicate that the offering of pigeons and doves was within the reach of all worshippers (Leviticus 1:14, 5:11). Many wild birds were eaten. The Patriarchs dined frequently on partridge, pigeon, guinea hen, goose, duck, quail, and sparrow. There are numerous biblical references to the hunting and trapping of fowl for the table (Job 18:8–10, Amos 3:5, Psalms 91:3, 124:7).

Water birds such as the duck were particularly abundant in the Nile Valley, where the Hebrews lived for four hundred years. A typical Egyptian banquet might feature several types of both wild and domesticated ducks and geese. These birds appeared less frequently in the drier climate of Israel, and were typically reserved for holidays there. Stuffed goose is the traditional centerpiece of the Chanukah feast. Later, the stuffed goose became a tradition of the St. Martin's Day feast.

The story of the flocks of quail provided for the Hebrews wandering in the Sinai (Numbers 11:32, Exodus 16:13) conforms to the still observable migratory patterns of this bird. During the European winter, flocks of quail migrate south over the Holy Land. Shifts in the wind often cause large numbers to fall onto the Sinai plains.

The introduction of chicken to the Holy Land cannot be accurately dated, though the bird is known to have originated among the Indus Valley civilizations. A painting from the tomb of Tutankhamun of about 1350 B.C. shows a typical barnyard rooster. This particular chicken was most likely an exotic, prized pet of the Pharaoh, not the common farm fixture it became.

Other sources claim the chicken arrived through the Persian trade routes a few centuries before the Christian era, a claim substantiated in the Bible. Although the Hebrew Scriptures do not mention the chicken, there are references to it in three of the Gospels (Matthew 26:34, Luke 13:34, 22:34, and Mark 14:30). By the eighth century B.C., the chicken was known to the Assyrians as "the bird that lays an egg every day." And the Romans were so familiar with the domestic chicken that dinners generally began with an egg course, a custom recalled in the Passover meal.

The cookbook of the Roman Apicius contains over twenty-five recipes for poultry. Grilling, stewing, and roasting with herbs and vegetables seem to have popular cooking methods for poultry, as they are today. Creamed chicken, chicken with wine sauces, and cold chicken salads were common Roman dishes. A banquet might have featured baked flamingo, ostrich, crane, and peacock. A small bird called the figpecker was a special delicacy, as its flesh was sweet from a diet of fruit.

Chicken With Sage in a Clay Pot

Sage grows wild in most Mediterranean countries and has since early times been used as a flavoring in cooking, fresh or dried, and as a salad green when fresh. The biblical type, *Salvia judaica,* is not available here, but our common sage can be substituted and has much the same taste.

1 4-pound chicken
2 tablespoons olive oil
$\frac{1}{2}$ cup parsley, minced
$\frac{1}{2}$ cup celery, chopped
1 tablespoon dried sage leaves, crumbled, or 3 tablespoons fresh

3 carrots, sliced
3 small turnips, sliced
12 tiny white onions, peeled
$\frac{1}{2}$ cup dry white wine (optional)
Salt and pepper to taste

Soak a clay pot in cool water for 25 minutes. Meanwhile, wash the chicken, pat dry, and rub with olive oil. Rub chicken cavity and outside skin with parsley and sage. Add salt and pepper. Place chicken in the pot, adding vegetables around inside and on top of chicken. Add wine if using. Cover with presoaked top of clay pot and place in a cold oven. Turn heat to 450°F and bake for 65 minutes. Remove the top to crisp the chicken for the final 10 minutes of cooking. During browning, remove the vegetables that are on top of the chicken. Replace after browning. Serve chicken from the pot, which will have rich juices on the bottom. Basic Barley or Millet complements the chicken and sauce.

Roast Chicken Stuffed With Fried Onions and Nuts

This tasty chicken roast recipe was translated from ancient Mesopotamian clay tablets. As with most ancient recipes, exact quantities of ingredients were not given, so we experimented to develop exact amounts.

1 teaspoon whole coriander seed
1 teaspoon fennel seed
1 teaspoon whole brown cumin seed
$\frac{1}{2}$ teaspoon whole celery seed
1 juniper berry
1 tablespoon dried pomegranate seed (optional)
Dash of cinnamon

8 large onions, finely chopped
3 tablespoons olive oil
5 tablespoons almonds or pine nuts
1 large roasting chicken
2 regular-size discs whole wheat pita bread
2 cups Basic Barley or Basic Bulghar
Salt to taste

In a mortar or clean coffee grinder, grind spices into a powder. Already ground spices may be substituted, but adjust quantities slightly upward. Reserve. Preheat oven to 350°.

In a skillet, sauté onions in 2 tablespoons olive oil until lightly golden. Drain onions on paper towels to remove as much oil as possible. Sauté nuts in remaining tablespoon oil. Drain as with onions. Combine ground spices, nuts, and onions, and stuff chicken with mixture, reserving $\frac{2}{3}$ cup for topping. Bake chicken in tightly covered dish or foil for $1\frac{1}{2}$ hours. Uncover and cook for an additional half hour, basting frequently with pan juices. To serve, line a warm serving dish with pita bread, spoon pan juices and warm, cooked grain on bread, and place chicken on top. Top with reserved onion, nut, and spice mixture. Salt to taste. Accompany with bowls of olives and a salad of mixed greens, and serve Fresh Berry Purée for desert.

Chicken Braised With Spinach and Prunes

This Persian combination is so delicious that it should be easy for you to get the family to eat both spinach and prunes. Queen Esther accomplished just such miracles of persuasion at the feasts she gave for King Ashasueras (Esther 5:4, 7:1).

1 large onion, sliced
½ teaspoon cinnamon
1 teaspoon turmeric
2 tablespoons chicken fat, oil, or butter
2 cloves garlic, minced
3 pounds chicken pieces
1 cup chicken stock
¼ cup tart grape juice, lemon juice, or vinegar
½ cup water

2 pounds fresh spinach or 20 ounces frozen (do not thaw)
10 pitted prunes
Dash of cumin
2 bunches scallions, chopped
½ teaspoon grated citron peel (optional)
Salt to taste
Walnut pieces

In a Dutch oven, sauté the onion with cinnamon and turmeric in oil, fat, or butter for 3 minutes. Add garlic. Then add chicken pieces and brown. Add all other ingredients (except salt and walnuts), cover, and simmer for 40 minutes or until

the chicken is cooked, adding more water if necessary. Salt
to taste. Add additional spices if desired. Garnish with walnut
pieces. Serve with lentils and rice, Basic Millet, and Honey
Cheesecake.

Spicy Braised Chicken With Millet

. . . also fowl were prepared for me . . .   Nehemiah 5:17–18

Nehemiah was appointed by the Persians to oversee the re-
construction of Jerusalem. By this time, Asian spices and the
Indus Valley chicken, introduced into the Holy Land by Persian trades, were becoming increasingly abundant.

6 cloves garlic
2 tablespoons fresh ginger,
   shredded
3 onions, chopped
1 tablespoon ground cumin
1 tablespoon ground coriander
$\frac{1}{2}$ cup water or stock
4 pounds chicken, cut in
   eighths
2 bay leaves
2 cinnamon sticks
$\frac{1}{2}$ tablespoon dill
1 tablespoon dried mint

1 tablespoon whole fennel
   seed
1 tablespoon ground cloves
1 teaspoon leaf saffron or
   turmeric (or both)
1 tablespoon citron
   preserve or orange
   marmalade
1 tablespoon honey
1 cup celery, chopped
1 tablespoon Fish Sauce
   (see page 73) (optional)
2 cups cooked millet (see
   Basic Recipe, page 103)
Salt to taste

In blender or mortar, mash the garlic, ginger, onion, cumin, and coriander. Reserve. Add a few tablespoons of water or stock if using a blender. Remove and discard skin from chicken. In a heavy stewing pot, brown chicken pieces in hot oil. Remove chicken and reserve. To the skillet, add the paste of garlic, onions, cumin, ginger, and coriander, and sauté, adding more oil if necessary. Add the remaining spices and continue frying gently. The mixture should exude a spicy aroma. Add the marmalade, honey, Fish Sauce, water or stock, and celery, stirring to blend.

Add chicken to spicy sauce in the stewing pot. Bring to a boil. Cover and turn down to a simmer. Cook for 20 to 30 minutes or until the chicken is tender. Salt lightly if desired. Serve the chicken atop the millet. As with all spicy dishes, this one is even better the second day. And it freezes well. Accompany with an Arugola Rose Salad and olives. Serve an assortment of dried fruits and nuts for dessert.

Baked Mustard Chicken Teimah

The golden-flowered mustard plant yielded abundant seeds and greens for the biblical kitchen. Jesus mentioned the beneficence of the mustard plant in a parable recorded in three of the Gospels (Matthew 17:20, Mark 4:31, and Luke 13:19).

4 pounds chicken parts,
   quartered or in eighths
4 tablespoons sharp mustard
1 tablespoon dried dill or
   thyme or 3 tablespoons
   fresh

$\frac{1}{2}$ cup whole wheat bread
   crumbs (see below)

Rub chicken pieces with mustard. Combine herb and bread crumbs. Coat chicken pieces with crumb mixture by dredging on a plate or dropping pieces into bag and shaking. Place chicken on a large, flat baking pan. Bake at 350°F for an hour. Covering the chicken will result in a "smothered" effect with gravy. Uncovered, the chicken will have a dry, crispy crust. Serve with Yogurt Soup, Baked Celery and Fennel, Onion Board, and Figs in Red Wine and Cream or Haroseth.

Whole wheat bread crumbs: For every $\frac{1}{2}$ cup, toast 4 slices of bread until crisp and dry. Tear in pieces and whirl through blender.

Greek Citrus Marinade for Chicken

This marinade uses some of the popular herbs of the Greeks, who took over the Holy Land from the Persians in 334 B.C.

4 pounds chicken pieces

MARINADE

1 cup olive oil
1 onion, thinly sliced
2 cloves garlic, crushed
½ cup orange juice
1 teaspoon orange or other citrus rind, grated

2 tablespoons ginger, shredded
2 teaspoons each rosemary and oregano
2 tablespoons vinegar
Salt to taste

To make marinade, combine all ingredients. Salt to taste. Marinate poultry at least one hour or as long as overnight. Bake, broil, or grill chicken. Boil marinade before serving as a sauce. Serve with Barley Herb Soup, Artichoke Hearts with Greens and Cream Cheese, Challah, and Fresh Berry Purée.

Roman Marinade for Grilled Chicken

Fermented fish sauces were among the most prized condiments of imperial Rome. The legacy of fish sauce is the frequent appearance of anchovies in contemporary Italian cooking.

4 pounds chicken pieces

MARINADE

1 teaspoon ground black pepper

5 tablespoons olive oil

4 cloves garlic, mashed

1 teaspoon celery seed

3 tablespoons Fish Sauce (see page 73)

2 teaspoons honey

$\frac{1}{2}$ teaspoon dry mustard

1 teaspoon each dried dill, mint, lovage, and rue if available (if using fresh herbs, triple the quantity)

In a large, shallow pan, combine the marinade ingredients and rub over the chicken pieces. Let sit at least an hour or as long as overnight, refrigerated. Turn pieces occasionally. Bake, broil, or grill chicken. Marinade should be boiled before serving as a sauce. This is also an excellent marinade for chunks of boneless chicken. Serve with other Roman-style foods such as Roman Asparagus, or Cruciferous Vegetable Bake.

Roman Chicken Salad With Fresh Peas

The Romans loved elaborate combinations. Fish, chicken, and veal might appear in one dish. This salad includes peas, a favorite Roman vegetable to which Apicius devoted an entire chapter of his cookbook.

2 cups romaine lettuce, shredded
2 cups cooked chicken meat, skin removed
1 cup fresh peas, steamed (use canned if necessary)
3 hard-boiled eggs

$\frac{1}{4}$ cup small pitted olives
3 to 5 anchovy fillets, chopped
1 tablespoon capers
1 cup celery, diced
4 tablespoons toasted almonds

Combine salad ingredients. Toss with vinaigrette dressing before serving.

VINAIGRETTE DRESSING

1 teaspoon honey
1 garlic clove, crushed (optional)
1 tablespoon prepared mustard

$\frac{1}{4}$ teaspoon celery seed
1 cup olive oil
$\frac{1}{2}$ cup vinegar
Salt to taste

Mash honey, garlic, mustard, and celery seed. Add oil, slowly, stirring constantly. Add vinegar. Salt to taste. Date Nut Bread or Honey Cheesecake will round out a light meal.

Duck in Grape Juice

. . . and I took the grapes and pressed them into Pharoah's cup . . .   Genesis 40:11

2 5-pound ducks (domestic or wild), 3 ducks if not using breast.

1½ cups whole wheat or barley flour

1 cup cooking oil

4 cups grape juice

½ cup red wine or red wine vinegar

Salt and pepper to taste

Cut up the ducks as you would a chicken. (The breast may be excluded from this dish if saving it is preferred.) Salt the duck and roll in the flour. In a large skillet, fry pieces in oil until golden brown. Pour off the oil and add the grape juice and wine or vinegar. Cook over medium heat for another 40 minutes or until duck is tender. Salt and pepper to taste. Serve with Basic Wheat Kernels, Coriander Relish, Endive With Olives and Raisins, and Watermelon in Ginger Wine.

Muscovy Duck With Quinces and Must Sauce

Our commercial ducklings are similar to the "fatted fowl" of King Solomon's table (1 Kings 4:23). The domestic Muscovy duck is a leaner bird than the Long Island duckling.

1 cup dry red wine

1 cup olive oil

2 Muscovy or wild ducks, dressed

2 tablespoons cinnamon

2 cups Must Sauce (see page 11)

5 quinces or hard pears

2 tablespoons freshly
  ground cumin
2 tablespoons freshly
  ground coriander

$\frac{1}{2}$ teaspoon salt

Combine wine and oil. Marinate ducks for one hour or more in this mixture. Preheat oven to 400°F. Combine spices and rub on ducks. Place ducks on rack with breast down. Place duck on rack in pan and add approximately $\frac{1}{4}$ cup water to prevent drippings from burning, but not so much as to steam the meat. Reduce heat immediately to 350°F. After a half hour, turn breast side up. Baste the duck with marinade. Roast a total of $1\frac{3}{4}$ to 2 hours, basting with marinade or pan drippings. The last basting should be with the Must Sauce. Turn off the oven when the bird is brown and done. Let rest 10 minutes before carving.

Prepare quinces or pears while duck is cooking. Cut the fruit into eighths, core, and seed. Remove a tablespoon of duck drippings from the pan and sauté the fruits with the drippings and salt in a small ovenproof dish. Cover and place in the oven for the last hour of cooking. Arrange ducks on a serving platter and surround with cooked fruit. Serve additional Must Sauce at the table. Basic Bulghar, with vegetables and Sourdough Fig Roll accompany this dish nicely.

Roast Duckling With Parsnips and Sour Plum Coriander Sauce

The sweet parsnip was a favorite food of antiquity and the Middle Ages right up to the ascendancy of the American potato in the seventeenth century. Parsnips and carrots are related and both are ancient vegetables. Originally the carrot was prized for its fragrant leaves. Through horticulture, the root became thick and succulent like the parsnip. The Sour Plum Coriander Sauce is Persian-style.

2 ducklings
Aromatic spices (bay, chervil, savory, thyme, garlic cloves, green onion tops, celery leaves)
3 cups parsnips, coarsely chopped

10 pearl onions
4 tablespoons honey
Salt to taste
1 cup Sour Plum Coriander Sauce (see page 95)

Boil the ducklings for 30 minutes in water to which the aromatic spices have been added. Remove duck, pat dry. Strain and degrease the duck stock. Reserve liquid and fat. Place ducks on rack in roasting pan, add the onions, and roast at 350°F for 1 hour. After 30 minutes add the parsnips. If a particularly brown skin is desired, coat ducks with honey for the last 10 minutes of cooking. Sauté cooked parsnips in a small skillet with onions, a tablespoon of duck drippings, and a tablespoon of honey. Parsnips should have a golden glaze to them. Salt to taste. Serve with Sour Plum Coriander Sauce, Basic Barley, and an unusual salad such as fresh arugola or mint with orange slices and radishes. Serve small squares of sesame halvah for dessert.

Grilled Breast of Duck With Rose Vinegar

Rose vinegar jams and sauces were luxury condiments in the ancient world. If you have a rose garden, you can prepare your own rose vinegar. Take fresh unsprayed petals. Place in a bottle and cover with white vinegar. Store several weeks before using. The process can be hastened by heating the vinegar to near boiling before combining with the petals. If you cannot obtain rose vinegar, flavor white vinegar with rose water, one teaspoon rose water to 3 tablespoons vinegar. Rose flavoring can overwhelm the uninitiated, so use sparingly and taste as you go along.

3 boneless duck breasts (preferably large, meaty ones) (chicken breasts may be substituted)

½ cup duck or chicken fat

2 cups rich duck or chicken stock

3 teaspoons to 3 tablespoons rose vinegar or 1 teaspoon rose water plus 2 tablespoons white vinegar (or to taste)

½ cup fresh parsley, chopped

Candied rose petals (optional)

Salt to taste

Skin the duck breasts. Sauté the skin in a small amount of duck fat until crisp. Chop and save for finished dish. Pound duck breasts into flat ¼-inch slabs. Brush with duck fat on both sides. Broil in the oven or over medium-hot charcoal 3 to 5 minutes per side.

Boil 2 cups of stock until reduced to approximately ⅔ cup. Add rose vinegar to taste. Reduce final mixture to about ½ cup. To serve, slather grilled duck breast with rose vinegar sauce and crisp skin pieces. Garnish with parsley and candied rose petals. Salt. Serve with Saffron Pilav, steamed spinach, crisp radish roses in a salad, and Goat Cheese Pancakes With Fennel Seed.

Pomegranate Walnut Duck or Chicken

Queen Esther gave two feasts to win the favor of the Persian king Ashasueras. Among the delicacies would have been Pomegranate Walnut Sauce on duck, chicken, or lamb. This sauce, the pride of the Persian kitchen, is a classic, and every Persian cook perfects an irresistible version. Experiment with the suggested spices and adjust the tartness and sweetness to your liking with fresh lemon and honey.

2 onions, chopped
4 tablespoons butter or oil
2 5-pound ducks or chickens
  cut in eighths
1 cup chicken stock (canned,
  if necessary)
1 cup pomegranate juice, fresh
  (see below), canned, or reconstituted syrup mixed
  with fresh lemon juice

2½ cups ground walnuts
½ teaspoon each cinnamon,
  clove, honey, pepper,
  cumin
Salt to taste
Pomegranate seed
Walnut halves

In a large skillet, sauté the chopped onions in butter or oil until they are golden brown. Remove onions and sauté the duck or chicken pieces. Return the onions to the skillet. Add stock and simmer for 15 minutes. Skim fat from surface. Add pomegranate juice, ground walnuts, and seasonings. Cover and simmer for 20 to 40 minutes or until poultry is cooked. Season further with salt if desired. Add water if sauce appears to be drying up. Serve on a bed of cooked barley or wheat. Garnish with fresh pomegranate seed and walnuts. The choice of canned, fresh, or reconstituted pomegranate juice will determine the need for honey and lemon. Canned juices will definitely need the tartness of fresh lemon.

FRESH POMEGRANATE JUICE

To extract juice from fresh pomegranates, first roll them along a hard surface to soften. Then cut in half and use an orange squeezer, or squeeze juice out by pressing halves with your hands over a bowl.

Be sure to try this recipe substituting 2 pounds of boneless lamb chunks for the duck or chicken. For a delightful Persian-style meal, begin with Cardoon Soup, serve the chicken, duck, or lamb with Basic Parched Wheat or Rice, Steamed Spinach, and baked apples or Pistachio Snow Sherbert for dessert.

Grilled Cornish Hens With Mint Garlic Marinade

We are substituting readily available Cornish hens for the pigeons, doves, partridges and other small birds enjoyed by people of the Bible, but use these other small birds if you wish.

½ cup olive oil
7 cloves garlic, crushed
2 tablespoons Fish Sauce
    (see page 73)
4 tablespoons honey
2 tablespoons vinegar

1 cup white wine
1 cup torn fresh mint leaves
    or ⅓ cup dried
6 Cornish game hens,
    halved or quartered
Fresh mint sprigs

Combine oil, garlic, Fish Sauce, honey, vinegar, wine, and mint leaves. Pour over cleaned birds and rub on all surfaces. Let stand at least an hour or as long as overnight, refrigerated. Prepare a charcoal fire. Drain marinade and reserve. Mount birds on skewers and grill for 45 minutes to an hour, turning every 15 minutes. In a saucepan, bring reserved marinade to a boil and simmer gently for a few minutes. Serve as a sauce. Garnish birds with fresh mint. Goes well with Basic Barley, Wheat Pilav, Whole Wheat Pita, a salad, beer, and fresh fruit for dessert.

Partridges or Cornish Hens With Nuts

. . . as one hunts a partridge in the mountains.   1 Samuel 26:20

1 cup white wine
½ cup olive oil plus 3 table-
    spoons poultry fat or oil
1 teaspoon ground
    coriander
2 tablespoons honey
5 shallots or green onions
1 bay leaf
⅓ cup vinegar
2 teaspoons dried or 2
    tablespoons fresh thyme

Salt to taste
6 partridges or Cornish
    game hens, quartered
1 onion, sliced
½ cup almonds, walnuts, or
    pistachios (or a combina-
    tion)
½ cup date, apricot, or grape
    brandy

Combine wine, oil, coriander, honey, shallots, bay leaf, vinegar, thyme, and salt. Marinate the birds for several hours, turning frequently. Remove and dry birds, reserving marinade. Brown onion in fat. Add birds and brown. Reduce heat, cover, and cook gently for about 20 to 30 minutes. Heat marinade in a separate pan. Toast the nuts. When the birds are tender, pour brandy over them. Ignite if the alcohol is to be burned away. Sprinkle the toasted nuts on top. Serve with toasted sourdough bread, Sweet and Sour Beets, a green salad with radishes, and Honeyed Cream.

Grilled Marinated Quail

So it was that quails came up at evening and covered the camp . . .   Exodus 16:13

6 to 10 quail, dressed
6 cloves garlic
6 juniper berries, cracked
4 scallions, chopped
1 cup dry white wine or
   apple juice

2 teaspoons cumin
2 teaspoons coriander seed
$\frac{1}{2}$ cup olive oil
5 tablespoons coriander
   leaves or parsley, finely
   chopped

In a shallow pan large enough to hold quail, combine all ingredients, except quail, into a marinade. Add the quail, coating all sides with sauce. Marinate quail for an hour, longer if desired. Drain, reserving marinade. Place marinade in a saucepan and bring to a boil. Place on grill to simmer while birds cook.

To grill quail, begin with breast side to the fire. Baste with cooked marinade. Grill for 2 to 3 minutes, turn, grill another minute or two. Breast meat should be firm but not dry. Serve marinade as sauce with quail. We recommend this dish as an appetizer. For a main course, double the quantities. Serve with Cucumbers Stuffed With Barley and Raisins, Goat Cheese, and Spinach Souffle.

Pigeon Pie   Serves 12–15

As a firstborn male child, Jesus was presented at the Temple in Jerusalem. Mary and Joseph, who made this pilgrimage to present the infant to God (Luke 2:22–24), also provided the offering of young pigeons, customary upon the birth of all children. This traditional pie, rich with nuts, eggs, and poultry, is still perfect for the celebration of a new arrival.

2½ pounds boneless pigeon or chicken meat (chicken thighs are close in texture to pigeon meat)
4 cloves garlic, mashed to a paste with salt (optional)
3 cups water
1 large onion, finely chopped
¾ cup parsley, chopped
1½ cups butter or almond oil
1 teaspoon ground coriander
¾ teaspoon ground ginger
½ teaspoon saffron threads, crushed (optional)
3 cinnamon sticks
2 cups blanched almonds
4 tablespoons honey
1¼ teaspoons ground cinnamon
⅓ cup grape juice or lemon juice
10 eggs
16 leaves of phyllo dough *
Salt and pepper to taste

Rub the poultry with the garlic paste if desired and let sit for 10 minutes. Then wipe off the garlic paste. In a large pot, put poultry, water, onion, parsley, ½ cup butter or oil, corian-

der, ginger, saffron, cinnamon sticks, salt, and pepper. Bring
to a boil, then simmer for 30 minutes to one hour. Remove
chicken meat and chop. Discard cinnamon sticks.

Sauté the almonds in a teaspoon of butter or oil and put
through grinder. Combine with honey and ground cinnamon.

Over high heat, reduce the liquid in which the chicken was
cooked to about 2 cups. Add grape or lemon juice. Whisk the
eggs and add to the simmering liquid, stirring constantly. Allow the eggs to cook to the consistency of yogurt. Transfer to
a bowl. The cinnamon-scented nuts, the egg custard, and the
spiced chicken meat compose the filling of the pie.

ASSEMBLING THE PIE

Have phyllo leaves ready with additional cup of melted butter
or oil nearby. Phyllo leaves should be covered with a damp
cloth to retain moisture. Work with a pastry brush or hands,
patting the leaves with butter or oil. Phyllo leaves are quite
fragile, but tears can be repaired by pinching dough together
with buttered fingers. In a 12-inch-round ovenproof skillet or
baking pan brushed with oil or butter, place 6 phyllo leaves,
each oiled. Overlap the sides. Fold two additional oiled phyllo
leaves in half and place in the center of pan. Sprinkle the
almond mixture over the phyllo leaves.

Spread half the egg mixture over the phyllo, followed by
the poultry pieces, then the last of the egg mixture. Fold the
overlapping phyllo pieces over this. Place the remaining phyllo
leaves, all oiled, over the top, tucking them around the sides
to cover. Bake in an oven preheated to 425°F for 20 minutes

---

*Phyllo leaves are well known in the cuisine of the Middle East and Mediterranean
area, but are not easily made by the inexperienced cook. Their preparation involves
highly skilled pastry making and separates the enthusiastic amateurs from the dedi-
cated professionals. If frozen phyllo leaves cannot be obtained make this as a quiche.

or until golden. Invert the pigeon pie on a cookie sheet, but do not remove original baking pan. Bake for an additional 10 minutes. Remove baking pan so top can toast to a crisp light gold. Serve pie on cookie sheet or reapply baking pan and flip over if necessary for storage. Before slicing, allow pie to cool slightly. Sprinkle with cinnamon and powdered sugar. Cut into diamond wedges and serve immediately. Olives, a mixed green salad, creamed spinach, and broccoli garnished with pine nuts and capers are good accompaniments.

Pigeon Quiche

4 basic Whole Wheat Pie
   Crusts (see page 175)

1 pigeon pie recipe (minus
   the phyllo leaves and minus 1 cup of butter)

The quantities in the pigeon pie recipe above will fill four pie shells. A quiche with a top crust would be most like the original recipe but will require eight times the basic pie crust recipe. Layer the fillings as instructed.

If more of a traditional quiche texture is desired, do not precook the eggs. Prepare the pies with nut-and-chicken fill-ing strewn on the bottom crust. Mix the eggs with the re-duced broth and pour over the filled pies. Bake at 350°F until egg custard is set. Serve with Onion, Olive, and Orange Salad, Yogurt Cheese Balls, and a selection of fresh vegetables.

Goose With Apple and Raisin Stuffing

Goose is the traditional Chanukah dinner. Its rich fat content symbolizes the extra oil that kept the Temple lamp burning when the Maccabees liberated Judaea from the pagan Greeks. This liberation is celebrated for the eight days of Chanukah.

1 12- to 14-pound goose

STUFFING

1 cup onion, minced (sautéed if desired)
3 cups apples, diced
7 cups whole wheat bread crumbs or cooked barley
1 cup seeded raisins
3 tablespoons honey

3 eggs, beaten
Water
Must Sauce, Sour Plum Coriander Sauce, or Candied Beet Preserve (see pages 11, 95, and 79)

Combine the stuffing ingredients and insert into the goose cavities. Sew up cavities or use skewers to close. Arrange stuffed goose on a rack. Prick the skin with a fork. Roast without basting for 15 minutes at 500°F. Then turn down oven to 350°F for remainder of cooking time. Total cooking time should be 20 minutes per pound based on weight of bird before stuffing. A little water may be added to the bottom of roasting pan to prevent the fat from burning. Garnish with Must Sauce, Sour Plum Coriander Sauce, or Candied Beet Preserve. Serve with Sumerian Watercress, Roman Asparagus, Arugola Rose Salad, and Honey Almond Paste.

HANDLING POULTRY FATS

Duck and other poultry fats obtained from roasting and boiling can be refrigerated and used for sautéing, baking, and enriching other foods. All poultry fats—duck, goose, and chicken—were highly regarded in ancient cooking, especially by the Hebrews, who were forbidden to use suet, lard, or butter with meat. Creamy poultry fat is an excellent texturizer in baking. In savory meat pies or casseroles, poultry fat adds a richness and depth to the flavor. When combined in equal parts with oil or butter, poultry fat has little effect on the taste of baked goods. Poultry fats are not recommended for those moderating cholesterol intake. Keep refrigerated.

Salty Sweet Eggs

In the Roman dinner, hors d'oeuvres generally included eggs.

$\frac{1}{4}$ cup onions, minced
Oil for deep frying
6 hard-cooked eggs
$\frac{1}{4}$ cup Date Syrup (see page 187)

4 tablespoons Fish Sauce
(see page 73)
Coriander leaves

In a medium-size skillet, sauté the onions in one tablespoon oil until golden crisp. Reserve onions and wipe skillet. Heat additional oil in skillet or pan suitable for deep-frying. Halve the hard-boiled eggs lengthwise and fry, yolk down, until the eggs are golden and blistered. Drain eggs yolk side up. Remove all but two tablespoons of oil from skillet. Add

Date Syrup, stir, and cook over low heat. Add Fish Sauce and let simmer for 5 minutes, stirring frequently. Pour sauce over fried eggs, sprinkle crisp onions on top, and garnish with coriander leaves. Serve with Barley Stew With Lentils and Chickpeas, Ashurey, or Chickpea Wheat Soup.

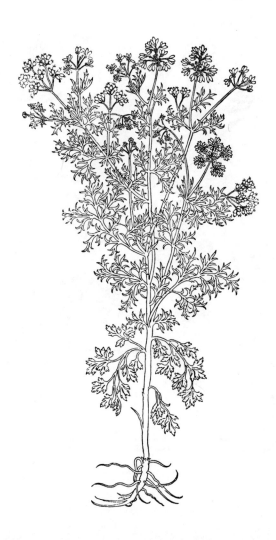

FISH

Jesus said to them, "Bring some of the fish which you have just caught."
Simon Peter went up and dragged the net to land, full of large fish, one
hundred and fifty-three, and although there were so many, the net was
not broken.
Jesus said to them, "Come and eat breakfast . . ."   John 21:10–12

✠   ✠   ✠   ✠

The fish predated the cross as the first symbol of the early Christian church. The Greek word for fish, *icthus,* was read as an acrostic for Jesus Christ, son of God, Savior. Because of this association and the many references to fish in the New Testament, it was a popular food with Christians.

The use of the fish as a symbol by the early Christian church harks back to the ancient Hebrew association of the fish with the coming of the Messiah. Some Hebrews believed the Messiah would actually come to earth as a big fish called the Leviathan. The eating of fish at the Sabbath meal evolved from the "pure suppers" at which fish was generally served as a symbol of hope for the future.

The Bible mentions four fishing methods still used in the Holy Land. Habukkuk 1:15 describes the use of the small hand net, casting a dragnet, and angling with a hook. Job 41:7 tells of spearing fish with a harpoon. Amos 4:2, Isaiah 19:8, Luke 5:4–9, and Matthew 13:47–50, 17:27 also mention these techniques.

Forty species of fish are found in the Holy Land. Twenty-two are particular to Israel and Syria. The Jordan River system, which includes the Sea of Galilee, has fourteen species of fish found nowhere else in the world, and was one of the richest fishing grounds of the ancient world. Indeed, the fishermen of Galilee controlled a lucrative business. The Sea of Galilee contains warm currents where large schools of fish congregate. Jesus apparently understood these currents, for he gave expert advice to his disciples on where to drop their nets (John 21:6). Carp, trout, and mullet were among the fish caught.

The Phoenicians supplied the Israelites with most of their marine fish in exchange for grain, as the Hebrews were not a seafaring people. The marine fish available at the Jerusalem fish gate mentioned in Nehemiah 3:3 and Zephaniah 1:10 would have included cod, sole, anchovies, herrings, gray mullet, red mullet, mackerel, tuna, and sea perch. Fish was preserved by drying and pickling.

The Romans were extraordinarily fond of sauces made with fermented fish pickles called *garum, liquamen,* and *muria.* All manner of fish and seafood were used in their preparation and there were many grades and variations. The cheapest, muria, was made from tuna fish.

These condiments compare to the inexpensive dark, brown Asian sauces of anchovy, shrimp, or oyster found today in Oriental markets. In Roman times, these condiments could be extremely expensive, particularly those made from the livers of red mullet, the culinary creation of Apicius, the Roman gourmet.

Fish With Honeycomb

*He [Jesus] said to them: Have you any food here? So they gave
him a piece of a broiled fish and some honeycomb,
and he took it and ate in their presence.*   Luke 24:41–43

Honey and fish are a unique and tasty combination, one of
the specific meals eaten by Jesus recorded in the Bible.
Here are some variations.

Broiled Fish With Honeycomb

per serving:

$\frac{1}{3}$ pound white, firm-fleshed   1 tablespoon honeycomb
   fish fillets or steaks   Vinegar or lemon juice
1 tablespoon olive oil

   Rub fish with olive oil and put into an oiled baking pan.
Bake at 350°F for 15 to 20 minutes or broil on low heat for 5
to 7 minutes on each side. Remove from heat and put a tablespoon of honeycomb on each fish steak or fillet. Turn up
broiler to high and put fish directly underneath heat to glaze.
Honey should caramelize into a light brown. Serve hot or
cold with vinegar or lemon juice. Accompany with Barley
Cakes.

Broiled Fish With Honey and Onions

Per serving:

1 small whole fish (such as bluefish, porgy, mullet, or trout)
1 tablespoon olive oil
1 cup red onion rings or other sweet onion, thinly sliced

1 tablespoon honey
1 tablespoon Fish Sauce (see page 73)
1 tablespoon fresh coriander leaves or parsley

Rub the fish with olive oil and place in a broiler pan with onion rings. Combine honey and Fish Sauce. Brush fish and onions with honey fish sauce. Broil for 5 to 7 minutes. Turn fish and onions; brush other side with same mixture. Broil until done. A crispy brown glaze should form on the fish and the onions. (The broiling of fish demands attention. The size of the fish and the temperature of the oven will determine the exact cooking times.) On a platter arrange fish and onions; sprinkle with coriander leaves. Serve with a tablespoon of honeycomb and Whole Wheat Barley Sourdough toast triangles.

Honey-fried Fish

1½ cups whole wheat flour
½ teaspoon salt
1¼ cups water
1 egg
2 pounds tuna, halibut, or
   cod steaks, cut into
   chunks

Oil for frying
1 tablespoon untoasted seas-
   ame, olive, or almond oil
2 tablespoons honey
2 to 3 tablespoons fresh
   toasted sesame seed

Sift flour and salt into a bowl. Make a well in the center. Combine water and egg, beat lightly, and gradually pour into the well of flour. Stir until smooth. Place 3 chunks of fish in a small bowl, pour batter over them. Set aside. Coat all the pieces in this manner. Heat frying oil in a skillet or wok. Fry fish pieces a few at a time until golden. Place fried fish pieces on paper towel to drain as they are removed from hot oil. After all pieces are fried, remove cooking oil and wipe pan clean. Heat a tablespoon of fresh oil in pan, add honey, and heat mixture thoroughly. Add fish and toss to coat with honey mixture. Remove to a serving plate and sprinkle with sesame seed. Serve with Basic Millet and Rose Apple Salad.

Grilled Saint Peter's Fish

Saint Peter's fish, or mushat, is believed to have been the fish that Jesus predicted would contain a shekel for taxes (Matthew 17:27). Other fish may be substituted.

6 small whole fish (such as mushat, sea bream, or mackerel)
1 to 2 tablespoons salt

$\frac{1}{2}$ cup parsley, chopped
2 onions, minced
$\frac{1}{2}$ cup olive oil
$\frac{1}{4}$ cup vinegar

Start charcoal fire or, alternatively, heat broiler. Slash sides of fish with a few diagonal cuts. Sprinkle cavity and outside of fish with salt. Let fish sit for 30 minutes. Place parsley and onion in fish cavity and close with toothpicks or by sewing. Brush fish with oil and place on an oiled grill. Combine the oil and vinegar and baste the fish. Do not cook too close to the flame, as fish can burn on the outside but still be raw inside. Grill or broil until first side is well browned before turning. Brown second side well. Serve with Fava Bean Soup and Tabbouleh Salad.

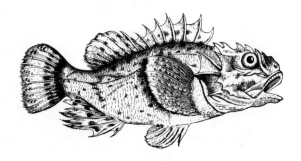

Broiled Trout With Anchovy Garlic Sauce

The Lord tells Jeremiah that Israel will be restored: "For I will bring them back into their land which I gave to their fathers. Behold, I will send for many fishermen," says the Lord "and they shall fish them . . ."   Jeremiah 16:16

6 cloves garlic
$\frac{1}{4}$ cup olive oil
3 tablespoons anchovy paste
    or small can of anchovy
    fillets
$\frac{1}{3}$ cup whole wheat bread
    crumbs (see page 36)

$\frac{1}{2}$ cup wine vinegar
$\frac{1}{2}$ teaspoon honey
$\frac{1}{2}$ cup water
6 small trout
Fresh coriander leaves

Briefly sauté the garlic in 2 tablespoons of the olive oil. Mash the anchovies, whole or paste, into the remaining oil with the bread crumbs, vinegar, and honey. Add the water. Simmer the sauce for 20 minutes. Keep warm while preparing fish.

Prepare fish by slathering the sides with the anchovy garlic sauce. Broil the fish over a high flame until done, about 5 minutes on each side. Alternatively, wrap in foil and bake for 20 minutes at 350°F. Serve fish with additional sauce and garnish with coriander. Suggested accompaniments: Persian Yogurt Soup With Meatballs, Whole Grains With Goat Cheese, and Honey Onion Sandwiches.

Sardines Grilled in Vine Leaves

Then as soon as they had come to land, they saw a fire of coals there, and fish laid on it and bread. John 21:9

1 cup olive oil
2 teaspoons salt
½ cup vinegar or lemon
  juice
1 tablespoon mustard
1 cup fresh herbs (dill,
  mint, thyme, bay,
  oregano, and basil)

3 to 4 pounds fresh sardines
  or 2 pounds fish fillets
12 to 40 vine leaves, fresh-
  blanched or preserved in
  brine
Hot mustard

Prepare a marinade of olive oil, salt, vinegar, mustard, and ½ cup of the fresh herbs. If using fillets, cut into 2-inch, narrow pieces. Marinate the sardines or fish fillets at least one hour, longer if possible. When ready to assemble, rinse the vine leaves and dry. Place one sardine or fish fillet on the corner of a vine leaf and roll up cigar-style, tucking the ends. Use two leaves if one is not enough. The packages may be secured with string or unwaxed dental floss if necessary. Grill over a charcoal fire, taking care not to excessively burn the leaves. Ten minutes should be enough time on a hot fire. Alternatively, steam or bake the stuffed vine leaves. To steam, use a vegetable steamer in a large pan with a tight-fitting lid. Steam for 20 minutes. To bake, place in a baking pan, add marinade, cover, and bake at 350°F for 30 minutes. Serve with mustard as a dip if steamed or grilled.

Egg-fried Fish With Two Cumins

Isaiah 28:27 compares the harvesting of two cumins. "For the black cummin is not threshed with a threshing sledge, nor is a cartwheel rolled over the cummin. But the black cumin is beaten out with a stick, and the cummin with a rod." Black cumin is also called black onion seed and *Nigella sativa.*

2 or 3 eggs, beaten
½ teaspoon salt
6 white fish fillets (such as trout, pike, flounder, sole, or bass)

Oil for frying
3 tablespoons black cumin seed

CUMIN SAUCE
1 tablespoon onion, chopped
½ teaspoon cumin
1 tablespoon honey
1 tablespoon ground coriander
Pinch of rosemary

Splash of vinegar
1 teaspoon olive oil
1 cup fish or vegetable stock or water mixed with 2 tablespoons Fish Sauce (see page 73)

To make sauce: Brown onions, vinegar, and spices in olive oil. Add stock, bring to a boil, and reduce liquid to one half.

To fry fish: Beat eggs with salt. Coat fish fillets in egg batter. Heat oil. Fry fillets in hot oil. Drain on paper towels. Arrange on platter and pour cumin sauce over fish. Sprinkle black cumin seed on top. Serve with Leeks and Cabbage, Endive With Olives and Raisins, French fried parsnips, and a radish salad.

Fried Fish in Radish Sauce

Radishes are one of the oldest vegetables of the Holy Land.
All parts of the plant were consumed. The leaves were
cooked as greens, the seeds were pressed for oil, and the
roots were eaten cooked or grated raw into vinegar for a
pungent dipping sauce.

6 fish fillets (such as flounder, sole, or cod)
1 teaspoon salt
1 cup whole wheat flour
1 cup oil for frying
$\frac{1}{4}$ cup sweet white wine

1 cup vegetable stock
$1\frac{1}{2}$ cups grated radish (mild
  white or red)
Coriander leaves
Chopped scallions
Parsley

Salt fish and coat with flour. In a large skillet heat oil and
fry fish until browned. Drain fried fish on paper towels. Discard oil from skillet; wipe skillet clean. In the skillet, combine
wine and vegetable stock and bring to a boil. Turn down to
a simmer. Add radish and stir. Add fried fish and heat briefly,
about 3 minutes. Garnish with coriander, scallions, and parsley. Serve with Basic Bulghar, Sprouted Essene Bread, and
Cinnamon Cheese.

Perch With Tahini

We remember the fish which we ate freely in Egypt.   Numbers 11:5

6 medium-size perch or
   other firm-fleshed white
   fish
Salt and pepper to taste
2 tablespoons vinegar
3 tablespoons parsley,
   chopped
1 tablespoon whole wheat
   bread crumbs

$\frac{1}{4}$ cup sesame oil
   (not Oriental)
2 medium onions, sliced
2 cloves garlic, chopped
$\frac{1}{2}$ cup tahini (sesame seed
   paste)

Score the fish on both sides, salt and pepper, and sprinkle with 1 tablespoon vinegar. Oil a baking pan and preheat the oven to 400°F. Mix two tablespoons of parsley with the bread crumbs and sprinkle over the inside of the oiled baking pan. In a skillet, gently fry the fish in 3 tablespoons of oil until golden on both sides. Reserve oil in skillet. Place fish in prepared baking pan.

In reserved oil, sauté the onions for 2 minutes. Add the garlic and continue sautéing for 2 minutes or until garlic is golden. Add remaining tablespoon of vinegar and tahini to the onions and mix well. Spoon over the fish. Bake for 15 minutes. Garnish with remaining tablespoon of parsley. Serve with Three Bean Soup, Yogurt With Fresh Herbs and Cucumbers, and Honey Cake.

Poached Fish With Capers

The caper is the pickled, unopened bud of the *Capparis spinosa* bush. In the Bible, the caper is called "desire" and is the plant referred to in Ecclesiastes 12:5: "and desire fails."

1 5-pound whole fish (such as weakfish or bluefish)
¼ cup olive oil
1 cup dry white wine
1 cup water
½ cup fresh dill or fennel or 3 tablespoons dried dill
4 scallions, minced

½ teaspoon salt (more to taste)
1 tablespoon ginger, shredded
1 teaspoon capers
Mayonnaise
Lettuce
Whole wheat pita

Lay the fish in a large pot and cover with the wine, oil, and water. Fish may be cut in half if a large enough pot is not available. Add dill, scallions, salt, and ginger. Cover and bring to a boil. Lower heat and simmer for 30 minutes. Place fish on a serving platter, pour poaching liquid over fish, and sprinkle capers on top. Serve with barley and Sumerian Watercress.

To serve cold, remove fish from liquid and fillet. Discard bones, skin, and head. Place fish pieces in a bowl, add capers, and pour cooking liquid over them. Refrigerate overnight. Serve the fish and capers in the jellied broth on lettuce with mayonnaise on the side. Accompany with Whole Wheat Sourdough Bread and Sweet Millet Balls for dessert.

Whitefish With Sorrel Sauce

Sorrel is one of the bitter herbs that fully deserves this appellation. The raw herb is not recommended for more than a garnish. When cooked, its tart, sour flavor is a good foil for fish.

¼ cup olive oil
2 onions, chopped
1 clove garlic, chopped
5 cups fresh sorrel leaves

2 pounds whitefish fillets or steaks (such as cod, halibut, or trout)
¾ cup water

Heat oil in heavy saucepan. Add onion and cook until almost transparent. Add garlic. Continue to cook until onion is transparent. Trim the sorrel leaves of their stems, wash, but do not dry. Add the wet sorrel leaves to the sautéed onion and wilt the leaves over medium heat until they have turned olive-green. Purée the cooked sorrel leaves in a blender.

Oil a dutch oven or wide pot. Place the fish fillets or steaks in the pot and top them with the sorrel sauce, using about half of the sauce. Add water to just below the fish. Cover and heat to boiling. Reduce heat and poach 3 to 6 minutes for fillets, 10 to 15 minutes for steaks. When fish is done, remove to a platter. Add the poaching liquid to the remaining sorrel sauce and pour sauce over the fish. Serve with Red Cabbage With Raisins, Yogurt and Mashed Parsnip, and Honey Fried Nuts.

Tuna With Apples and Raisins

The Men of Tyre were the Phoenicians who sold Mediterranean specialties such as tuna at the Jerusalem fish gate. The arrival of fresh ocean catches on Saturdays was irresistible to some fish-loving Israelites, who were then admonished for making purchases on the Sabbath (Nehemiah 13:16).

2 pounds tuna steaks or 3
   cans tuna
1 tablespoon butter
½ cup sweet red wine

6 pieces whole wheat toast
   (optional)
Parsley or coriander leaves

SAUCE

¼ cup raisins
¼ cup grated apple
2 tablespoons sweet red
   wine
2 tablespoons olive oil
1 tablespoon vinegar
¼ teaspoon ground coriander

1 teaspoon celery seed
½ teaspoon oregano
1 cup fish stock or water
   mixed with 2 tablespoons
   Fish Sauce (see page 73)
Salt to taste

In a saucepan, combine sauce ingredients and bring to a boil. Lower heat and simmer for 25 minutes.

In a baking pan, dot tuna steaks with butter and sprinkle with wine. Bake for approximately 20 minutes until meat is white and flaky, but not dry. Arrange on platter and serve with the sauce. Garnish with parsley or coriander leaves.

If using canned tuna, drain and rinse. Add to sauce after it has simmered for 25 minutes. Serve on toast. Garnish with parsley or coriander leaves. Serve with Vegetable Soup With Whole Grains, and Yogurt Drinks such as Grape and Carob.

Tuna Salad With Fresh Fennel

Whatever in the water has fins and scales, whether in the seas or in the rivers—that you may eat.   Leviticus 11:9

3 7-ounce cans tuna or 2
  pounds fresh
Large outer lettuce leaves
  (optional)
1 large fennel bulb,
  chopped into bite-size
  pieces

$\frac{1}{2}$ cup raisins
2 dill pickles, chopped
2 crisp apples, chopped
Romaine lettuce leaves
Sliced radishes

DRESSING

$\frac{1}{2}$ cup olive oil
1 tablespoon mustard
1 teaspoon honey

Pinch of celery seed
Salt to taste
$\frac{1}{4}$ cup vinegar

Wrap fresh tuna in lettuce leaves or foil (prick small holes throughout if using foil) and steam for 30 minutes in a bamboo or metal vegetable steamer over boiling water. If using canned tuna, rinse and drain. Break fish into small chunks. In a small bowl, combine oil, mustard, honey, celery seed, and salt. Beat in vinegar. Into a salad bowl, place chopped fennel, raisins, pickle, apple, and tuna. Pour dressing over salad and toss. Substitute a light dressing if desired. Serve on romaine lettuce leaves and top with radish slices. Accompany with Chickpea Wheat Soup or Cream of Barley Soup and Carob Spicery Seed Bread.

Pickled Fish

Pickled fish was a favorite of the ancient world. Egyptians, Romans, Greeks, and Hebrews were all fond of this flavorful preservation method. Today, availability of fresh, frozen, and canned fish has limited the need for pickling methods and recipes. Still, pickled fish is an excellent low-calorie main dish or appetizer.

2 pounds pike or other whitefish, filleted
4 small onions, sliced
2 cups water
Salt and pepper
2 bay leaves
1 cup white vinegar

2 teaspoons mixed pickling spices (or prepare your own using dill seed, mustard seed, coriander seed, black peppercorns, and cloves)
1 citron or lemon, sliced
1 tablespoon honey

Wash fish carefully under cold water. Put fish, 2 onions, 2 cups water, salt, and pepper into a saucepan. Bring to a boil, then gently poach fish for 10 to 20 minutes or until tender but not falling apart. Place fish in a jar. Strain broth and mix with the rest of the sliced onions, bay leaves, vinegar, spices, lemon slices, and honey. Bring this mixture to a boil and pour into the jar. Cover and shake to distribute the ingredients. Let marinate in refrigerator a day before serving. Serve with Whole Wheat Sourdough Bread, cheese and fruit.

Salt Fish Vegetable Soup

Dried, salted fish was a staple of the ancient world. It makes an excellent and convenient stock for soups.

8 cups boiling water
½ pound dried, salted fish
(such as cod; also known
as bacalao)
2 tablespoons olive oil
2 cloves garlic, mashed
3 tablespoons dried seasonings (thyme, mustard
seed, mint, pepper,
cumin, coriander, bay
leaf)

1 cup onions, chopped
1 cup white turnips, sliced
1 cup green peas
1 cup cabbage, shredded
½ cup carrots, sliced
½ cup bulghar wheat

Pour 2 cups boiling water over dried fish and let sit for 15 minutes or until tender. Discard water and rinse the fish under running water. Break or cut up fish into small pieces, removing bones. Heat olive oil in a soup pot and add the fish and onion. Brown, stirring constantly. Add garlic and seasonings. Stir, heating through. Add the vegetables, turning a few times in the hot oil. Add cracked bulghar wheat and 6 more cups boiling water. Cover and simmer until vegetables are crunchy-tender, about 20 minutes. Accompany with Matzah, Pressed Coriander Cheese, and Raisin, Barley, and Apricot Pudding.

Tabbouleh Codfish Cakes

Fish, meat, and fowl were preserved by drying and salting.

1 pound dried, salted fish (such as cod; also known as bacalao)	3 tablespoons parsley, minced
6 cups boiling water	2 small onions, minced
2 cups tabbouleh (small-grained bulghar wheat)	2 eggs, beaten
	2 teaspoons cumin
	$\frac{1}{4}$ cup oil

Place fish in a bowl and cover with 2 cups boiling water. Put tabbouleh in a separate bowl with 4 cups boiling water. Let both sit for an hour.

Remove skin and any stray bones from fish. Cut or shred fish into very small pieces. Drain wheat and squeeze out excess water. Combine fish, bulghar wheat, parsley, onion, eggs, and cumin. Run through food processor to achieve a fine mash if possible. Form mixture into balls or patties and fry in oil until outsides are golden and crusty. Turn carefully. Serve with Hot Garlic Sauce (see page 164). Egyptian-Style Fava Bean Soup and Arugola Rose Salad are suggested accompaniments.

Sabbath Fish Balls

Boned fish cakes have been a Sabbath specialty for millen-iums. This ancient recipe comes from the Ethiopian Jewish community, which reckons its descent to the liason of King Solomon and the Queen of Sheba (1 Kings 10:1–13).

2 pounds poached, steamed,
  or baked whitefish fillets
4 slices whole wheat bread
3 onions, finely chopped
6 tablespoons butter
6 tablespoons whole wheat
  flour
2 teaspoons salt
½ teaspoon pepper
1½ teaspoons dry mustard

1 cup milk
4 medium dill pickles,
  minced, or ½ cup pickle
  relish
1 tablespoon pickle juice
2 eggs, beaten
½ cup whole wheat bread
  crumbs or matzah meal
Vegetable oil for frying

Flake the cooked fish fillets and set aside. In a large bowl, soak the bread slices in ¾ cup milk and mash into a paste or put through the blender until smooth. In a medium skillet, sauté the onion in butter until soft. Blend in flour, salt, pepper, and mustard. Add ¼ cup milk and stir. Remove from heat. Add to bread and milk mash along with pickle, pickle juice, and flaked fish. When blended, form the mixture into small balls between palms of hands. Dip in beaten egg and coat with bread crumbs or matzah meal. Fry in hot oil until golden. Serve fish balls with an herbed yogurt. During Passover, these fish balls are always made with matzah meal.

Fishballs make an elegant appetizer to any roasted lamb, beef, or chicken meal. For a light luncheon, serve them with Cardoon Soup and Cold Creamed Beet Yogurt Drink.

Fish Sauce

Fermented fish sauces are called for in nearly every one of Apicius's Roman gourmet recipes and the classical historian Pliny ridiculed his extravagance with these condiments. Many similar products are available today in Asian groceries. The anchovy sauce used in Thai and Vietnamese cuisines is probably most like the fish sauce used in ancient Roman cooking. Ask for "Nuoc Nam" or simply "fish sauce." When using, reduce or delete other sources of salt; small amounts blend well into any nondairy savory sauce. The Roman word *garum* is similar to the Greek word for shrimp, suggesting a main ingredient in one of the versions of this condiment. These may have resembled the Oriental shrimp pastes or even the Chinese oyster sauces.

From the basis of fermented fish, the sauces were embellished with herbs, vegetables, wine, fruit sugars, and exotic spices. If this all sounds unbearable to your modern palate, try reading the ingredients on a bottle of Worcestershire sauce. This English specialty is a latter-day descendant of the fine Roman fish sauces and illustrates perfectly how the "fishiness" disappears into a pungent, spicy, but very pleasant flavor.

If Oriental fish sauce is not available, make one with a 2-ounce can of anchovies drained and ¾ cup wine or water.

Combine the anchovies and wine in a small saucepan. Simmer for 10 minutes. Purée the sauce in a blender or hand mash with mortar. Hand-mashed sauce will require straining. Refrigerate.

Recipes using fish sauce include Roman Beef Sauté With Ginger and Onions, Salty Sweet Eggs, Grilled Cornish Hens With Mint Garlic Marinade, Roman Cruciferous Vegetable Bake, and Leeks and Cabbage.

FRUITS AND VEGETABLES

And God said: "See I have given you every herb that yields seed which is on the face of the earth and every tree whose fruit yields seed, to you it shall be for food.   Genesis 1:29

F ruits and vegetables were the only food God provided in the Garden of Eden, thought to have been in Mesopotamia because of the description of its rivers in Genesis 2:10–14. Religious vegetarians base their practice on this vision of Paradise.

The Bible mentions over one hundred plants by name. Terms such as firstfruits (Exodus 22:19) included all the bounty of the harvest—grains and vegetables as well as the figs, grapes, and pomegranates that made up the bulk of the Holy Land fruit crop.

Many of the vegetables eaten in biblical times were primitive varieties of the ones we eat today. The Hebrew Scriptures are relatively unspecific as to the then common vegetables, and much of our information comes from Egyptian, Mesopotamian, and later Greek and Roman records. Plants with edible stalks are simply called herbs in the Hebrew Scriptures, although this group included celery, asparagus, and beets as well as seasoning agents such as cumin, juniper, and bay. The

New Testament mentions six vegetables specifically: mustard, thistles, mint, rue, dill, and sprouted grain.

Fruits figure more prominently in biblical lore than vegetables. There were many species of grapes, figs, and pomegranates. An ancient image of peace and earthly happiness was that of one sitting under one's own vine and fig tree (Isaiah 36:16). The time and skill needed to grow quality fruit gave rise to metaphors of patience, nurturance, sweetness, accomplishment, and failure. In fact, Jesus frequently used images of fig and grape cultivation in His parables.

Apple was a generic name used for various round fruits such as golden apples (apricot), must apples (quince), and Persian apples (citron). Cherries, apricots, peaches, and plums came to the Holy Land via Persia and Mesopotamia. By the time of the Christian era, these fruits were cultivated throughout the Mediterranean area.

The excesses of wine were well known in the biblical world. Indeed, scholars have speculated that the forbidden fruit of Eden was actually a grape. What other fruit, they ask, could so easily have tempted the first couple to disobey God? But if alcohol drove man to sin, the grape was not the lone culprit, for the ancients were proficient at obtaining spirits from figs, dates, and grains. And the wine obtained was generally diluted with water and often spiced with cinnamon, honey, and herbs.

The Roman cookbooks of Apicius provide elaborate examples of vegetable stews and spicy cooked-fruit compotes. Salads, combining the green leaves of many wild plants and herbs as well as lettuce, were normally dressed with oil and vinegar. Candied vegetables were very popular, and fruits were sometimes preserved in honey and grape syrup. Further, the arts of preserving in brine and vinegar were well established in the ancient world and the dill pickle is as old as the Pyramids.

Roman Asparagus

This first-century recipe calls for grinding the fresh asparagus rather than steaming or boiling. The Romans called this type of dish a *patina.*

3 pounds fresh asparagus
1 cup white wine
3 shallots or scallions, chopped
2 tablespoons olive oil
Pinch of celery seed and savory

$\frac{1}{3}$ cup beef, chicken, or vegetable stock
1 tablespoon butter
3 eggs, beaten
Salt and pepper to taste
Fresh coriander leaves

Put fresh asparagus through food grinder or processor to achieve a thick mash. Sprinkle with half of the wine. Sauté shallots in a tablespoon of the olive oil until transparent. Add celery seed and savory and stir briefly. Add asparagus, stock, oil, butter, and wine. Simmer, stirring frequently. As mixture begins to bubble, stir in eggs, keeping heat low. Salt and pepper to taste and moisten with more wine or stock as needed. Garnish with fresh coriander leaves and serve with warm pita bread.

Sweet-and-Sour Beets on a Bed of Beet Greens

Beets were among the produce of the Babylonian king Merodach-Baladan's garden.

2 bunches fresh beets with bright green tops
2 tablespoons olive or almond oil
1 tablespoon honey
$\frac{1}{3}$ cup vinegar
$\frac{1}{2}$ teaspoon orange rind, chopped
$\frac{1}{4}$ teaspoon ground cinnamon
Salt to taste
Dash of cumin
Fresh coriander or parsley
Yogurt

Cut green tops from beets, reserving an inch of stem on the beet roots to prevent excessive "bleeding." Wash the beet greens and chop, then sauté in 1 tablespoon oil for 5 minutes. Reserve.

Boil whole beet roots until tender, about 25 minutes. Drain, reserving cooking liquid. Peel and chop beets. In a saucepan, combine honey, vinegar, orange rind, remaining oil, cinnamon, salt, cumin and ¼ cup reserved cooking liquid. Simmer over low heat for 10 minutes, stirring frequently. Add the cooked beets to sauce and warm thoroughly. On a serving platter, make a layer of beet greens and spoon beets on top. Garnish with coriander and yogurt. This colorful dish may be served hot or cold.

Candied Beet Preserve

Candied vegetables were favorites of the ancient world, and this colorful preserve was traditionally eaten on Rosh Hashanah, the autumnal Jewish New Year, for a sweet new year.

8 cups beets, peeled and quartered
1 teaspoon salt
½ cup water
4 cups honey
5 teaspoons ground ginger

2 lemons, thinly sliced
2 cups walnuts or almonds, coarsely chopped

In a large pot, cook beets with salt in water to cover until almost tender. Drain, cool, and cut beets into julienne strips or cubes. In a large saucepan, combine honey, ginger, and ½ cup water. Bring to a boil and add beets and lemon. Lower heat and simmer about one hour, or until beets begin to have a transparent look and mixture is extremely thick. Add nuts and cook for another 5 minutes. Pour into sterilized glass jars. Store in a cool dark place. Alternatively, store in refrigerator or freezer if sterilized containers are not used. Makes approximately 7 8-ounce containers. Serve with turkey, chicken, or Roman Ham.

Cardoons and Artichokes

The cardoon, an early form of the artichoke, is thought to be the thistle of Genesis 3:18. Cardoons look like celery and taste like artichokes. They make an excellent addition to all vegetable and meat stocks, possessing taste-enhancing qualities like the artichoke. Cardoons are beginning to appear in supermarkets. They are hardy perennial plants, remarkably easy to grow. (see p. 204)

COOKING CARDOONS OR ARTICHOKES

Trim the tough, stringy cardoon fibers and the artichoke spikes if desired. Bring a large pot of water to a boil. Add a splash of vinegar or lemon juice, then the cardoons or artichokes. Cardoon pieces need 30 to 90 minutes of cooking to become tender. Cardoon pieces may be substituted for artichoke hearts in all recipes, if precooked. Artichokes cook in 30 to 40 minutes.

Artichoke Hearts With Spinach and Cream Cheese

12 ounces cream cheese at
   room temperature
$\frac{1}{4}$ cup milk
3 shallots or scallions,
   chopped
1 tablespoon butter
12 ounces cooked spinach
   (frozen may be used),
   well drained and chopped

12 ounces cooked artichoke
   hearts or cardoon pieces
$\frac{1}{8}$ teaspoon dried thyme or $\frac{1}{4}$
   teaspoon fresh thyme
Salt and pepper to taste

Mash cream cheese and milk together in the bottom of a baking dish. Reserve. In a small skillet, sauté shallots or scallions in butter until golden. In the baking dish, place sautéed onions, spinach, artichoke pieces, thyme, salt, and pepper, and toss with the cream cheese mixture. Cover and bake 30 minutes at 350°F until hot and bubbly. Serve with whole wheat toast and a fruit salad.

Cardoon Soup

2 pounds cardoons
1 large onion, chopped
2 tablespoons olive or vegetable oil
4 tablespoons whole wheat flour

8 cups chicken or beef stock (bouillon cubes may be used)
2 teaspoons salt
3 tablespoons vinegar
Coriander leaves

Wash cardoons, remove large prickly strings and green outer edges. Chop into small pieces. In a large soup pot, sauté the onion in oil. When onion is transparent, add cardoon pieces and stir. Add flour and stir constantly for 3 minutes. Add stock, salt, and vinegar. Cover and simmer for 1½ hours, or until cardoon pieces are tender. Garnish with coriander leaves.

Roman Cruciferous Vegetable Bake

The cabbage family are called cruciferous vegetables because their flower patterns form the shape of a cross. They were popular vegetables of imperial Rome.

1 small onion, chopped
1 bay leaf, crumbled
2 tablespoons olive oil
1 or 2 cloves garlic
$\frac{1}{2}$ pound red cabbage
$\frac{1}{2}$ pound white cabbage
1 pound kale
1 head broccoli
1 quince or tart apple

$\frac{1}{4}$ cup parsley, chopped
$1\frac{1}{2}$ cups dry white wine or
  apple juice
1 tablespoon honey (less if
  using apple juice)
1 tablespoon Fish Sauce
  (see page 73)
Salt to taste

In a large skillet, sauté onion and crumbled bay leaf in olive oil until onion is transparent. Add garlic at the last minute to brown. Add the cabbages and kale, broken up into bite-size pieces. Stir for 5 minutes. Add all other ingredients. Place mixture in an ovenproof casserole. Bake at 350°F for one hour. Shorten or lengthen the cooking time, depending on how vegetables are preferred. Let stand for 10 minutes before serving.

Red Cabbage With Raisins

Apicius, the Roman gourmet, recommended this combination.

$\frac{1}{2}$ cup raisins
$\frac{1}{2}$ cup apple or grape juice
1 large red cabbage
3 tablespoons vinegar
1 tablespoon honey

Pinch of cinnamon
Salt and pepper to taste
1 tablespoon butter
  (optional)

Soak the raisins in the fruit juice for at least 2 hours. Cut the cabbage into strips, discarding the tough inner core. Oil a baking pan and place the cabbage in it. Sprinkle with vinegar. Cover and bake at 350°F for 30 minutes. Add the raisins, fruit juice, honey, and cinnamon. Bake another 15 minutes, more if a softer texture is preferred. Salt and pepper to taste. Alternatively, sauté cabbage briefly in butter in a Dutch oven. Cover and simmer, stirring occasionally for 15 minutes. Add other ingredients and simmer another 20 minutes.

Baked Celery and Fennel

Celery and its relative, fennel, are believed to have originated in Egypt, where they were called "the doorkeepers to heaven." Fennel adds interest to the familiar celery.

2 fennel bulbs, cut into
  ½-inch pieces
1 head celery, cut into
  ½-inch pieces
2 tablespoons butter

3 tablespoons olive oil
Salt to taste
Sprinkling of caraway seed
  (optional)

Sauté fennel and celery in the butter and olive oil. Transfer to a baking pan, cover, and cook 30 to 45 minutes in an oven preheated to 350°F. Salt to taste. Sprinkle with caraway seed.

Cucumbers Stuffed With Barley and Raisins

. . . in a garden of cucumbers . . .   Isaiah 1:8

6 cucumbers
1 onion, chopped
2 tablespoons olive oil
1 cup cooked barley (see
   Basic Recipe, page 101)
1 cup raisins, soaked for 1
   hour in water and drained
1 tablespoon vinegar

2 tablespoons fresh mint or
   2 teaspoons dried
$\frac{1}{4}$ teaspoon cinnamon
Salt and pepper to taste
$1\frac{1}{2}$ cups water
7 tablespoons Garlic Mint
   Relish (optional, see below)

Halve the cucumbers lengthwise and remove seeds, form-
ing pockets. Peel cucumbers only if they are waxed. Set aside.
Sauté onion until golden in oil. Add barley, soaked raisins,
vinegar, mint, cinnamon, and salt and pepper to taste. Stuff
cucumber pockets with barley-raisin mixture and place in a
large pot. Add water, cover, and bring to a boil. Simmer for
35 minutes or until cucumbers are tender. Garnish with Garlic
Mint Relish if desired.

Quinces, apples, and fennel bulbs may also be stuffed with
this mixture and cooked in this manner.

GARLIC MINT RELISH

3 cloves garlic
4 tablespoons fresh mint or
   4 teaspoons dried

1 teaspoon salt
2 tablespoons vinegar

Crush garlic, mint, and salt with a mortar and pestle or in
a small bowl with the back of a fork. Add vinegar. Sprinkle
over stuffed vegetables before serving.

Endive With Olives and Raisins

This unusual vegetable combination includes three of the most abundant foods in the Holy Land. You may substitute other greens, such as escarole, spinach, or red lettuce, for the endive.

4 cloves garlic
$\frac{1}{3}$ cup olive oil
2 pounds endive, torn into
   bite-size pieces
$\frac{1}{2}$ cup chicken stock
$\frac{1}{4}$ cup raisins

$\frac{1}{4}$ cup oil-cured olives, pitted
   and chopped
2 tablespoons capers
Toasted almonds
Salt to taste

In a large skillet, sauté garlic cloves in oil until golden. Discard the cloves. Add the endive and continue to sauté for 5 minutes. Add the chicken stock, raisins, olives, and capers. Simmer for 15 minutes, stirring frequently. Garnish with almonds. Taste before salting, as olives can be quite salty.

Biblical Herb Soup or Soup of the Seven Sorrows

Seven bitter herbs go into this soup to symbolize the seven sorrows of Mary, the mother of Jesus. The Feast of the Seven Sorrows, an ancient repast, occurs on the sixth Friday of Lent.

$\frac{1}{4}$ cup olive oil
$\frac{1}{4}$ cup whole wheat pastry
 flour
2 large onions, chopped
2 cloves garlic
1 bunch parsley
1 bunch radish greens
1 cup sorrel leaves or
 bunch of spinach
1 large endive
1 bunch mustard greens
 (use $\frac{1}{2}$ bunch if large)

1 bunch turnip greens (use
 $\frac{1}{2}$ bunch if large)
1 bunch coriander
(Beet greens, chards, collard
 greens, carrot tops, or
 other available greens
 may be substituted for
 those listed).
6 cups water
1 teaspoon salt
1 tablespoon vinegar
 (optional)

In a soup pot, heat oil and slowly add flour, stirring frequently until mixture is a rich brown. Add onions and garlic. Cook over low heat until onion is soft and brown, stirring frequently. Wash and chop or tear the greens. Add to the soup pot and cover with the liquid (which should rise above the vegetables). Add more water if necessary. Salt. Simmer for at least 30 minutes. Taste and add more salt and the vinegar if desired. Sorrel broth, which is sold in supermarkets as Schav, can be used instead of part of the water and sorrel.

The exact cooking time varies with individual tastes. These strong-flavored vegetables are often preferred well stewed. Two hours' cooking time is a general maximum. Croutons are a nice garnish.

This soup makes a fine light meal with bread and cheese. Although it is traditionally vegetarian, the addition of ham bones, meat, chicken, and their stocks does make an excellent, hearty soup.

Leeks and Cabbage

Leeks appear to have been the favorite onion of ancient Egypt. Among the medicinal uses suggested in an ancient papyrus scroll is in treatment of human bites. Leeks are still a favorite around the Mediterranean and can be easily grown in home gardens.

5 cups water
Salt and pepper to taste
1 cabbage, quartered
4 to 6 leeks
1 tablespoon Fish Sauce
  (see page 73)

1 teaspoon cumin
1 teaspoon dill
1 teaspoon coriander
1 tablespoon oil
1 tablespoon vinegar

Bring to a boil several cups of salted water. Plunge the quartered cabbage and leeks into the boiling water for 10 minutes. Drain and chop coarsely. Mix remaining ingredients and place all into an oiled baking pan. Bake at 350°F for 20 minutes. Serve with lamb or grilled chicken. Lettuce can be substituted for cabbage (romaine is especially good).

Grilled Leeks and Scallions

In the Holy Land, certain areas were renowned for their onions. The city Ashkelon lent its name to its favorite onion, the scallion.

3 to 6 scallions per person *or*
  2 to 4 leeks per person

Olive oil

Rub the cleaned whole scallions and/or leeks with olive oil and place on the side of a grill over a charcoal fire, away from the direct flame. Some like their onions charred, but for us the perfect grilled onion is tender, cooked through with little dark brown patches on the outside. Leeks will need extra time on the grill. This dish is a simple and delicious complement to any grilled food, especially shish kebabs. Wrap meat and onions up in a fresh pita and serve with a pungent mustard.

Poached Lotus Roots

Lotus roots were the potatoes of ancient Egypt. Look for them in Oriental vegetable markets.

$1\frac{1}{2}$ pounds lotus roots, as young as possible

3 tablespoons oil

2 teaspoons roasted cumin seed

2 teaspoons fennel seed

1 teaspoon powdered coriander seed

2 tablespoons mustard seed

Salt to taste

2 cups water

Scrape and peel the lotus roots as one would a potato. Cut into slices. Heat the oil, add all ingredients, and sauté for 3 minutes. Pour in 2 cups water and bring to a boil. Cover and simmer for at least one hour. Taste. Lotus roots are hard and full of little holes, and older roots in particular will need more cooking time.

Marinated Lotus Root Salad

Many of the biblical references to lilies are in fact to the lotus, a water lily, or to the onion, which is a member of the lily family.

$1\frac{1}{2}$ pounds lotus roots

Vinaigrette dressing (see Arugola Rose Salad, page 92)

Peel and scrape the lotus roots. Cut into thin slices. Boil until tender, about one hour (older roots take longer to cook). Toss with vinaigrette and let marinate for several hours.

Honey-Onion Sandwiches

Across the Fertile Crescent, the standard workingman's lunch appears to have been bread with onions. Here is a delicious version of this ancient combination. It should be made a day ahead of eating.

2 large mild onions, sliced
1 cup water
$\frac{1}{4}$ cup honey
1 cup mayonnaise
$1\frac{1}{2}$ teaspoons sharp prepared mustard

Fresh whole wheat bread
1 cup parsley, chopped
Salt and pepper to taste

Place the onions in a bowl. In a small saucepan, bring the water and honey to a boil and pour over the onions. To make the onions crisp, store them in the refrigerator with a layer of ice on top. When ready to use, drain and pat dry. Mix the mayonnaise and mustard, spread on slices of whole wheat bread, and top with onions. Sprinkle chopped parsley over the onions. Salt and pepper to taste. Serve with beer and a bowl of smoked almonds.

Whole Baked Onions

We remember . . . we ate freely in Egypt . . . the leeks, the onions and the garlic.   Numbers 11:5

1 large onion per serving
3 tablespoons rich stock or
   1 bouillon cube per
   onion

Large cabbage leaves
   (optional)

Peel each onion and remove enough of the top to wedge a bouillon cube in the leaves. Wrap in aluminum foil and bake one hour at 350°F. Alternatively, spoon stock onto each onion and wrap tightly. These onions are delicious roasted in the coals.

To bake in cabbage leaves: Prepare onions with bouillon cubes or stock as above. Wrap each in a large cabbage leaf and pack into a baking dish. Cover and bake one hour at 350°F. Serve this low-calorie treat instead of a potato.

Sumerian Watercress

Watercress is thought to have been one of the bitter herbs of Exodus 12:8. Ancient watercress seeds have been found in Egypt, and watercress was among the plants listed in the Babylonian records. Sesame seed was a customary garnish for Mesopotamian foods.

2 bunches fresh watercress	**1 tablespoon vinegar**
3 tablespoons sesame seed	**Dash of cumin**
½ cup chicken broth	**Dash of coriander**
1 tablespoon honey	**Salt to taste**

Wash watercress and trim only rough or dirty stems. Prepare 4 to 6 bundles, one for each serving. Lay stems together and tie with string. Bring a large pot of water to a boil and plunge in the tied bundles of watercress. Let boil for a scant 2 or 3 minutes. Remove and immediately place under cool running water to refresh. When cool, press out water thoroughly so that bundles will retain their shape when the strings are removed.

Heat sesame seeds in heavy frying pan without oil. Stir constantly to prevent burning. Seeds should begin to jump and pop. Remove from heat and crush seeds with mortar and pestle or nut grinder. Combine with broth, honey, vinegar, cumin, coriander, and salt. Alternatively, place toasted seed in blender with dressing ingredients. Pour dressing over the watercress bundles. Serve in separate bowls or alongside meat, poultry, or fish.

Arugola Rose Salad

Arugola and zucchini were well known by Roman times.

1 bunch radishes
2 medium zucchini
1 cucumber

1 bunch arugola
Handful of rose petals,
    freshly picked (optional)

VINAIGRETTE DRESSING
1 tablespoon honey
3 tablespoons olive oil
3 tablespoons vinegar

1 teaspoon prepared mus-
    tard
Salt to taste

Wash and dry the vegetables and rose petals. Chop the radishes, zucchini, and cucumber into round pieces. Tear the arugola into bite-size pieces. In the bottom of a large salad bowl, mix the dressing ingredients. Add the vegetables and petals and toss.

Fresh Fig and Grape Salad

The fig tree puts forth her green figs, and the vine with the tender grapes give a good smell. Rise up, my love, my fair one, and come away.   Song of Solomon 2:13

1 head fresh red-leaf lettuce
    or other leaf lettuce
15 fresh figs, quartered

1 cup seedless grapes,
    halved if desired

MINT CAPER DRESSING
$\frac{3}{4}$ cup olive oil
$\frac{1}{4}$ cup lemon juice or
    vinegar

1 tablespoon capers
1 tablespoon fresh mint,
    chopped

Wash and dry lettuce. Arrange lettuce leaves on individual plates, top with figs, then grapes. Mix dressing ingredients and pour over salad or serve alongside.

Onion, Olive, and Orange Salad

The Hebrews seem to have cultivated citrus fruit throughout the Mediterranean, although its exact origin is obscure. One citrus fruit, the *ethrog,* was eventually incorporated into the ritual celebration of Sukkoth, the autumn harvest festival.

4 oranges, peeled, cut up, and seeded
1 red onion, thinly sliced

1 cup halved black olives (pitted and chopped; oil cured are best)

Combine oranges, onion, and olives. Chill if desired. This unusual combination does not require a dressing.

Rose Apple Salad

Refresh me with apples, for I am lovesick.   Song of Solomon 2:5

5 large tart apples (such as Granny Smith)
Juice of one lemon
4 tablespoons honey
2 teaspoons rose water (more to taste)

Candied rose petals
Mint leaves
Crushed ice

Grate unpeeled apples and place in a bowl. Add lemon juice and honey; then add rose water. Chill. Garnish with rose petals and mint and serve on top of a bed of fresh snow or crushed ice. Serve with roast lamb, chicken, or grilled fish and as a side dish with Basic Fresh Curd and Yogurt Cheeses and Whole Wheat Sourdough Bread. Rose Apple Salad is an excellent light dessert or snack for children.

Coriander Relish

When the hay is removed and the tender grass shows itself
And the herbs of the mountains are gathered in . . .   Proverbs 27:25

1 clove garlic
1 cup coriander leaves,
   chopped
½ teaspoon cumin powder
½ teaspoon salt

1 tablespoon vinegar
8 ounces yogurt or 4
   ounces ground walnuts
   mixed with ½ cup water

Mash garlic, coriander, cumin, salt, and vinegar together in a mortar or whirl through blender. Stir in yogurt or walnuts to make a smooth paste. Serve immediately or refrigerate and serve within three hours of preparation. Serve this with grilled chicken, roast lamb, poached fish, or mixed with mayonnaise as a sandwich spread.

Sour Plum Coriander Sauce

This Persian-style sauce is easy to make in a blender.

2 pounds fresh plums
2 cups water
$\frac{1}{4}$ teaspoon salt
3 tablespoons coriander
   leaves, chopped (more to taste)

1 clove garlic
$\frac{1}{4}$ cup shelled walnuts

   Seed plums and place in a large saucepan with water and salt. Boil for 20 minutes, stirring occasionally and adding more water if necessary. Turn off heat and let cool. Place sauce in blender with coriander leaves, garlic, and walnuts. Blend until creamy. Return to saucepan and heat to boiling. Cool. Store in refrigerator. This sauce is an excellent marinade and basting sauce for grilled chicken and meats.

Grape Leaves

The Bible mentions grape leaves only to relate a prohibition against them. Manoah's wife is forbidden to eat them while pregnant with Samson (Judges 13:14), but grape leaves, like fig leaves, were commonly eaten.

40 to 200 fresh grape leaves	$\frac{1}{2}$ cup regular salt
4 quarts water	$\frac{1}{2}$ cup pickling salt

Pick grape leaves early in the summer. Cut off stems and wash, then stack in piles of twenty leaves each, shiny side up. Roll up and tie with a string.

Measure about 2 quarts water, add $\frac{1}{2}$ cup salt, and bring to a boil. Drop the grape leaves bundles into the boiling water, a few at a time. Return to a boil and blanch for 3 minutes. Turn the rolls over as they boil so they will blanch evenly. Lift out and drain.

Prepare a brine of 2 cups water to $\frac{1}{4}$ cup pickling salt. Pack the blanched bundles in sterilized jars and pour the brine over them. Remove air bubbles and seal. Wash in fresh water before using.

Alternatively, wrap blanched leaves in freezer bags and store in freezer until ready to use. Besides being excellent for stuffings, grape leaves can be added to soups, stews, and stir-fry dishes.

Homemade Olives

Can a fig tree, my brethren, bear olives . . . ?   James 3:12

2 pounds fresh olives $\frac{1}{3}$ cup pickling salt
6 quarts water   3 tablespoons olive oil

Fresh olives are generally available in the fall. Pick those without bruises. In each olive cut a few slits with a knife or mash slightly with a flat object. The skin must be broken. Place olives in a deep bowl and cover with cold water. Place a plate on top to weigh olives down and keep them under the water. Change water every day for 4 days.

Prepare a brine of one quart water with $\frac{1}{3}$ cup pickling salt. Drain olives and put into clean sterilized jars. Cover olives with brine. Add a few drops of olive oil to the top of each brine-filled jar. Cap jars and store for 6 weeks before using. Rinse in cold water before serving. Discard overly soft olives, if any.

WHOLE GRAINS
AND BEANS

Whole grains and beans were the sustaining daily food of the people of the Holy Land. The wild grasses that yield barley and wheat can still be found growing on the sunny hillsides as they did millenniums ago. The beginning of grain cultivation involved a complicated merging of primitive technologies: plows and hoes were needed to plant, pottery to store, and millstones to grind the grain. This process is considered the beginning of civilization, for as a result mankind developed a steady food supply and, in turn, stable communities. Flanking the Holy Land, Mesopotamia and Egypt possessed unique river systems that, by serving as means of irrigation, enabled the development of grain empires.

The irrigation methods of the ancient world have barely been surpassed today. Mesopotamia, now Iraq, was once the most fecund grain-producing area in the world. Though its vast network of irrigation canals required careful management to prevent silting, deterioration of the system came only after a series of wars that destroyed the central administration of the grain industry and general resolve of the populace. The fertility of the region has never been restored to the levels of ancient times.

Ancient people expected to see grain at every meal in one form or another: green, boiled and parched, soaked and roasted, malted into beers, and baked into puddings, flans, and casseroles. Grain was sprouted, pounded, dried, crushed, and reconstituted. But bread was a luxury, not a convenience food, in ancient times, because hours of laborious pounding, grinding, and sifting were necessary to make flour. Centuries passed before fine flours became common and inexpensive. In the meantime, the average family of biblical times ate a wide variety of porridges, pilavs, soups, and parched-grain salads.

The people of the Bible saw the grace of God in an abundant grain harvest and feared His wrath would manifest itself in a famine. Hence, the close timing of grain harvests and religious festivals was not a coincidence; it was considered the spiritual rhythm of the universe. Rituals involving grain were part of the holidays. The barley harvest was in early spring, at the time of Passover; seven weeks later the wheat was harvested at Shavout (Pentecost). Sheaves of wheat were laid upon the altar of God in Thanksgiving. This identification with God's purposes and food production was fundamental to the ancient mind. Nothing in nature was thought random or accidental.

By the time of Jesus, grain trading was conducted throughout the Roman empire on a massive scale. Wheat was preferred in trade, since barley is heavier and therefore more difficult to transport. The farming of barley therefore declined, though its hardiness ensured that a steady local supply could be grown on the poorer soils. Millet was also widely cultivated during the time of Jesus in southern Europe, though it never achieved the popularity of barley or wheat in the Holy Land (it is mentioned only once in the Bible, as an ingredient of Ezekiel bread).

Beans and peas, the pulses, are frequently named in the same sentence with grains in the Bible, and were often accompaniments to grain at the biblical table. They are one of the few vegetables mentioned specifically in the Bible, underscoring their importance as a primary source of vegetable protein and nourishment. Petrified beans were found at the famous excavations of Jarmo in northern Iraq and in the Egyptian tombs at Thebes. Beans were included among the foods forbidden at Passover because they were considered to go through the same leavening process as grain. Ancient Egyptian priests had especially complicated restrictions surrounding the consumption of lentils, peas, favas, and chickpeas, yet Egyptian royalty was often buried with a supply of beans in their final resting chamber.

Basic Barley

These six ephahs of barley he gave me; for he said to me, "Do not go empty handed to your mother-in-law."   Ruth 3:17

Barley is one of the world's hardiest grains and today is used primarily for brewing beer. Native to the Holy Land, it can grow in cold climates, atop mountains, and in unirrigated soil, and is found around the globe in such diverse places as Scotland, the Himalayas, and Korea. Barley has long been known for its easy digestibility. Avoid the pearled barley in favor of the browner, whole-grained varieties generally available in health food stores. Barley and millet are often toasted before boiling water is added to cook them (see page 103). Ancient cooking records suggest that roasted barley was made into a brown all-purpose condiment similar to soy sauce.

1 cup barley (hulled is commonly available)	3 cups water Pinch of salt

Rinse barley and place in medium saucepan with water and salt. Bring to a boil, then simmer for one hour undisturbed. Barley will expand to three times its dry volume. Serve with butter or gravy in place of rice.

Barley Water

This ancient preparation is reputed to clear the complexion and forestall wrinkles, but at the very least it makes a nutritious drink.

1 cup barley 8 cups water	$\frac{1}{2}$ cup honey (more to taste) Pinch of salt

Rinse barley and place in soup kettle with water and salt. Bring to a boil and simmer a minimum of 2 hours, a maximum of 24 hours, adding more water as necessary to keep water level at about 5 cups. Longer cooking times will result in a thicker barley water. Strain the barley and discard. Flavor the barley water with honey. Serve chilled.

Basic Millet

. . . take for yourself wheat, barley, beans, lentils, millet . . .   Ezekiel 4:9

Whole millet is a hardy, fiber-rich cereal available at most health food stores. Like barley, it does not contain sufficient gluten to produce yeasted breads which require wheat. On the other hand, whole millet cooks in 20 to 40 minutes as opposed to the hour needed for barley and the four to six hours needed for whole wheat kernels. In ancient times, this represented a significant saving in firewood. Millet, a native of Africa, was widely grown in the Roman empire at the beginning of the Christian era. Its brief popularity was eclipsed by the gains of rice, a newcomer from the Orient.

$\frac{1}{4}$ cup hulled millet seed $\frac{1}{4}$ teaspoon salt
$1\frac{1}{2}$ to 2 cups boiling water
   or stock

   Rinse millet seed. Place in saucepan with boiling water or stock and cook over a low flame for 20 minutes, covered. Add salt and let stand another 20 minutes. The seeds will open. Alternatively, toast millet in a large skillet until it is lightly browned. Add boiling liquid and proceed as above. Use less liquid for a crisper grain; full amount for a softer grain. This recipe makes about 2 cups of cooked millet.

Basic Wheat Kernels

Wheat is the queen of grains. Its high gluten content makes it the first choice in fine baking. Indeed, the light, moist, and flaky textures we associate with the best breads and cakes are simply not possible with other flours. The white flour we see everyday in the grocery would have been an incomparable luxury to the people of the Bible.

Ancient wheats were such extremely hard-headed low yielding little kernels that humanity soon set itself to developing better strains and milling methods, technologies which developed over many centuries. Preparing a pot of whole wheat kernels, or wheat berries as they are often called, will illustrate this property, for even after soaking overnight wheat kernels need 4 to 6 hours of cooking. The homemaker of antiquity often kept a pot of wheat kernels about the fire, soaking, simmering, only occasionally boiling, for 24 hours or more. The thickened milky cooking liquid was taken regularly from this pot (and replenished) to be used in puddings, porridges, sauces, and beverages.

1 cup whole wheat berries   **Pinch of salt**
4 cups water

In a large saucepan with lid, place wheat berries, water, and salt. Bring to a boil, cover, and simmer 4 to 6 hours or until tender. Add more water as necessary.

Basic Cracked Wheat (Bulghar or Tabbouleh)

So she sat beside the reapers, and he passed parched grains to her; and she ate and was satisfied and kept some back.
Ruth 2:14

Cracked wheat, bulghar wheat, and tabbouleh refer to whole wheat kernels that have been boiled, dried, and cracked. The cracking of the wheat results in fine, medium, and coarse grains. Thus treated the wheat will soften quickly when boiling water is added and the grains allowed to soak. The coarser grains may be cooked briefly.

Other grains and even beans may be treated this way, but such products are generally available only in health food stores, while bulghar and tabbouleh are becoming common in supermarkets. To the biblical cook, this process, though initially laborious, resulted in a quick cooking wheat with better storage properties than the fresh grain. Cracked wheat retains all the fiber of whole wheat and as a nutritious convenience food has not been surpassed in modern technology. It is sometimes called parched wheat. This recipe makes about 4 cups of prepared bulghar.

1 cup bulghar wheat   3 cups boiling water

Pour boiling water over bulghar wheat and let stand 30 minutes until wheat is tender and fluffy. Drain if necessary.

Bulghar or Cracked Wheat Pilav

1 cup bulghar or cracked
    wheat (coarse grains are
    best for pilav)
1 to 3 teaspoons spices
    (cumin, coriander seed,
    minced garlic, ground
    pomegranate seed, dried
    thyme) (optional)

2 tablespoons butter
2 cups water or stock
    (chicken, beef, lamb, or
    vegetable)
Salt to taste
Parsley
Coriander leaves

Sauté grain and spices in butter for 3 minutes. Add stock
or water. Bring to a boil, cover, reduce heat, and simmer for
10 minutes. Turn off heat and let pilav sit for 15 minutes. Salt
to taste. Fluff with fork and garnish with greens. Serve with
meat, chicken, or fish.

Cream of Barley Soup

*"Now they came to Bethlehem at the beginning of barley har-
vest."* (Ruth 1:22).

Ruth and Naomi availed themselves of the ancient charity
that allowed the poor to glean the barley fields after reap-
ing.

$\frac{3}{4}$ cup barley
5 cups vegetable, beef,
    chicken stock or bouillon
    cubes*
$\frac{1}{2}$ cup heavy cream

Salt to taste
$\frac{1}{4}$ cup celery leaves
Fresh parsley or coriander
    leaves

Wash the barley in warm water. Cook in 4 cups of the stock with the celery leaves for 2½ hours. Mash the cooked barley by hand (avoid using a blender or food processor, as this tends to create a gummy texture). Add the remaining cup of stock. Before serving, heat barley and add the cream. Salt to taste. Garnish with parsley or coriander leaves.

*This dish depends on a good stock to give it definition. Bouillon cubes are a last resort if fresh stock is unavailable.

Barley Herb Soup

Simmered barley herb broth was a health tonic to the ancients, taken for upset stomachs, fevers, and postfestival hangovers.

½ cup barley
4 cups vegetable or chicken
  stock
1 to 4 tablespoons of fresh
  or dried herbs (thyme,
  pennyroyal, parsley, celery leaves, coriander
leaves, savory, chervil,
  mint)*
1 onion, chopped
3 tablespoons chopped
  celery
2 tablespoons butter or oil
Salt to taste

Rinse the barley and put into a soup pot with the stock. Add the herbs. Bring to a boil, then simmer gently for 5 hours. Remove scum from the broth as it surfaces. Add water as necessary. Sauté the onion and celery in butter until brown and caramelized. Add to soup pot. Salt to taste and garnish with fresh herbs.

*1 tablespoon fresh herb = 1 teaspoon dried

Vegetable Soup With Whole Grains

When Daniel was a captive in the Babylonian court of King Nebuchadnezzar, he asked to be given a vegetarian diet so as to avoid the rich food and non-Kosher meat. The king's stewards were afraid they would be blamed if Daniel became weak. To reassure them, Daniel and his three Hebrew companions conducted an experiment for ten days, eating only vegetables. "And at the end of ten days their countenance appeared better and fatter in flesh than all the young men who ate the portion of the king's delicacies." (Daniel 1:8–16).

4 tablespoons butter or
   vegetable oil
4 carrots, chopped
3 onions, chopped
2 parsnips, chopped
2 stalks celery, chopped
2 quarts water or stock
1 cup barley, millet, or
   bulghar wheat

1 teaspoon salt
½ pound beet greens, spinach, or red lettuce leaves
1 cup cooked chickpeas
Chopped parsley and/or
   coriander leaves

In a large soup pot, sauté the chopped vegetables in the butter or oil until lightly cooked. Add the water. Add the barley, millet, or bulghar. Add salt. Simmer for at least one hour or until grain is tender. During the last 15 minutes of cooking add the chickpeas and shred the washed greens into the soup. Garnish with parsley and/or coriander leaves.

Barley Stew With Lentils

Whole grains and beans, eaten together, were a primary source of complete protein, B vitamins, and dietary fiber for the people of the Holy Land. Since modern nutritional science affirms the health value of these foods, serve them with confidence any time of day.

$\frac{1}{3}$ cup onion, chopped
$\frac{1}{2}$ cup celery, chopped
$\frac{1}{2}$ cup carrots, chopped
5 tablespoons butter
5 cups water or stock
1 cup dried lentils, picked over and washed

$\frac{1}{2}$ cup barley
$\frac{1}{8}$ teaspoon rosemary
2 teaspoons salt
2 teaspoons ground cumin
$\frac{1}{2}$ pound beet greens or spinach

In a large soup pot, sauté the chopped onion, celery, and carrots in the butter. Add the water or stock, lentils, barley, rosemary, salt, and cumin. Bring to a boil, turn down heat, and cook until lentils and barley are tender, about one hour. Remove scum as it forms. Add greens for the last 15 minutes of cooking.

Cold Grain and Bean Salads

. . . a land of wheat and barley . . .   Deuteronomy 8:8

3 cups freshly cooked pearl barley, bulghar wheat, whole wheat kernels, or millet (see Basic Recipes, pages 101–105) *or*
3 cups freshly cooked warm

lentils, chickpeas, or fava beans
(See page 118, Three Bean Soup, for basic information)

SALAD

½ cup parsley and/or coriander leaves, chopped
1 bunch scallions, chopped
2 cucumbers, chopped
1 bulb fennel, chopped, or
  4 stalks celery, chopped

1 bunch radishes, chopped
½ cup pitted black olives
½ cup raisins or date pieces
3 hard-boiled eggs, sliced
  (optional)

DRESSING

1 clove garlic (optional)
1 heaping tablespoon horseradish mustard
1 to 2 teaspoons honey
2 tablespoons fresh herbs
  (dill, thyme, oregano,
  mint, chives, savory, and
  chervil)
1 tablespoon cumin

½ cup olive oil
¼ cup vinegar, tart grape
  juice, or lemon juice
  (more to taste)
Salt to taste
Garnishes (optional): Poppy
  or sesame seeds, crum-
  bled goat cheese, romaine
  lettuce

Rub a large salad bowl with the cut clove of garlic and
discard. In the salad bowl, prepare the dressing: Mix mustard,
honey, herbs, and spices. Add oil, then add vinegar or tart
juice, varying proportions as desired. Salt to taste. Mix warm
grains or beans with dressing. Allow to cool. Add salad ingredients and toss. Chill if desired. Garnish with poppy or sesame seed, goat cheese, or romaine lettuce. Proportions can
be varied to taste. These salads are a meal in themselves as
well as excellent snacks and side dishes.

Tabbouleh Salad

*So the children of Israel camped on Gilgal, and kept the Pass-
over on the fourteenth day of the month at twilight on the plains
of Jericho. And they ate of the produce of the land on the day
after the Passover, unleavened bread and parched grain on the
same day.*   Joshua 5:10–11

1 cup fine-grained bulghar
wheat
3 cups boiling water
1 bunch scallions, finely
chopped
2 cups parsley, chopped
4 tablespoons vinegar
(lemon juice can be substituted)

$\frac{1}{2}$ cup radishes, chopped
Salt to taste
3 tablespoons olive oil
1 teaspoon sharp mustard
Romaine lettuce leaves

In a large bowl, cover the tabbouleh with boiling water.
Let soak for 30 minutes or until tender. Drain the wheat and
combine with all other ingredients except lettuce leaves. Marinate and chill for several hours, or overnight, in refrigerator.
Heap salad on a platter and arrange lettuce leaves around it
so that they may be used as scoops. This is an excellent
luncheon dish.

Millet Pilav

Millet is high in protein and fiber.

1½ cups hulled millet seed
3 tablespoons butter or oil
1 medium onion, sliced into
   fine rings
1 stick cinnamon, about 2
   inches long
1 teaspoon ground cumin

1 teaspoon ground
   coriander
1 clove garlic
2 tablespoons raisins
1 teaspoon salt or to taste
3 cups boiling water

Roast millet as suggested in Basic Recipe (see page 103) and set aside. In a heavy 2-quart pot, melt the butter over a medium flame. Add the onion, cinnamon, spices, and garlic. Stir and sauté for about 5 minutes or until the onion is translucent. Add the raisins. Stir and sauté for another 5 minutes, lightly caramelizing the onion. Add the roasted millet, salt to taste, and 2¾ cups of water. Bring to a boil, cover, and turn down the heat. Simmer for 20 to 30 minutes. Pour ¼ cup boiling water over the millet, stir quickly, and continue to cook on low heat for 10 minutes. Turn heat off and let the pot sit, covered, for 15 minutes. Can be served with lamb or chicken.

Saffron Pilav

Spikenard and saffron,
Calamus and cinnamon
myrrh and aloes
with all the chief spices   Song of Solomon 4:14

$\frac{1}{4}$ cup fresh orange peel, thinly sliced
3 cups boiling water
$\frac{1}{2}$ teaspoon saffron threads
2 tablespoons warm water
2 tablespoons oil or melted butter
1 medium onion, sliced
$\frac{1}{2}$ teaspoon each ground cumin, ground coriander, and cinnamon, more to taste
1 teaspoon salt
$\frac{1}{4}$ cup pine nuts
3 cups cooked barley, cooked millet, or soaked bulghar (see Basic Recipes, pages 101–105)

Cut orange peel into small slivers. Pour one cup of boiling water over slivers. Let sit for 5 minutes. Drain and repeat. Set aside. Place the saffron threads in a bowl and add the warm water. Set aside for up to 4 hours.

In a skillet, heat the oil or butter and sauté the onion. As the onion becomes transparent, add the cumin, coriander, cinnamon, and salt. Sauté, stirring constantly, for 3 minutes. Add the orange peel and the pine nuts and stir for 2 minutes. Add the cooked grain and the saffron-tinted water. Add 4 tablespoons boiling water, more if necessary, to keep mixture from burning. Work over moderate (not hot) flame. Cover skillet and steam for a few minutes. When thoroughly heated, remove cover to let any remaining water evaporate.

Whole Grains With Goat Cheese and Chickpeas

. . . earthen vessels and wheat, barley and flour, parched grain and beans, lentils, and parched seeds, honey and curds, sheep and cheese of the herd, for David and the people who were with him to eat. 2 Samuel 17:28–29

½ cup olive oil
1 teaspoon sharp mustard
⅓ cup fresh lemon juice or vinegar
Salt and pepper to taste
3 cups softened bulghar, or cooked barley, millet, or wheat kernels (see Basic Recipes, pages 101–105)
½ cup parsley, chopped
½ cup fresh mint leaves (or to taste)

1 bunch green onions, chopped
2 cups cooked chickpeas (16-ounce can)
4 ounces feta cheese, chopped into chunks
2 tablespoons black olives, chopped
Lettuce leaves

Whisk olive oil, mustard, and vinegar or lemon juice, into a dressing. In a salad bowl, combine grains, parsley, mint, green onions, chickpeas, cheese, and olives. Add dressing. Season with salt and pepper. Let marinate and chill overnight if possible. Arrange lettuce leaves so they can be used as scoops. Serve with grapes and unleavened barley bread.

Chickpea Wheat Soup

This hearty porridge is typical of what people ate for breakfast in the ancient Holy Land. It is traditionally served on Saint Lucy's Day, December 13.

$\frac{1}{2}$ cup dried chickpeas or 1 cup cooked chickpeas (canned may be used)
1 cup whole wheat kernels
1 bay leaf

$\frac{1}{4}$ teaspoon cinnamon (more to taste)
1 to 2 teaspoons salt
8 cups water
Honey to taste

Soak the dried chickpeas and wheat kernels overnight in separate containers. In a soup pot, place the drained wheat kernels, bay leaf, cinnamon, salt, and approximately 8 cups of fresh water. Bring to a boil, then simmer for 2 hours. Add the soaked chickpeas and continue simmering for 1 to 2 hours or until the wheat is tender. (Canned chickpeas should be added to the simmering wheat after 3 hours.) Add more water as necessary. Serve with honey.

Esau's Pottage

Esau's Pottage is one of the most famous recipes in history, and to this day various simmered red-lentil dishes are known as Esau's Pottage in the Bible lands. Esau, like his father Isaac, was susceptible to the blandishments of a well-prepared stew. The improvident Esau is victimized by the manipulation of his brother and mother in Genesis, Chapters 25–27.

1 onion, chopped
1 tablespoon olive oil
$\frac{1}{2}$ teaspoon ground cumin
$\frac{1}{2}$ teaspoon ground coriander
2 cloves garlic, minced
3 cups beef or vegetable
  stock, or water mixed
  with beef or vegetable
  bouillon cubes

1 cup red lentils
$\frac{1}{2}$ pound spinach
  (optional)
salt to taste

In a large stewing pot, sauté the chopped onion in the olive oil with the cumin and coriander. Add the garlic at the last moment and brown. Add lentils and stock. Stir well and bring to a boil. Reduce heat. Simmer 45 minutes until lentils are tender; cook 10 minutes longer if necessary. Add spinach 15 minutes before serving. Salt to taste.

Fava Bean Soup

3 cups shelled fresh or frozen fava beans or 2 cups
  dried, hulled fava beans
4 cups chicken, beef, lamb,
  or vegetable stock
2 cloves garlic
1 teaspoon ground cumin

1 teaspoon ground corian-
  der
1 teaspoon ground pome-
  granate seed (optional)
1 tablespoon olive oil
$\frac{1}{2}$ cup fresh coriander or
  parsley, chopped

Fresh or frozen beans: Shell the beans if fresh or defrost if frozen. In a soup pot, simmer beans with stock for 30 minutes. Add garlic, cumin, coriander, and pomegranate seed. Continue cooking for 30 minutes to an hour or until beans are tender.

Dried beans: Soak dried beans for one or two days. In a soup pot cover dried beans with water and bring to a boil. Simmer for one hour. Add garlic, cumin, coriander, and pomegranate seed. Continue to simmer another 30 minutes to an hour or until tender.

Separate cooked beans from liquid with slotted spoon and mash by hand with potato masher or put in blender. Add oil to mashed beans and return to cooking liquid. Garnish with fresh coriander or parsley.

EGYPTIAN-STYLE FAVA BEAN SOUP

Hard-boil an egg for each portion. Sauté an onion and 6 cloves garlic in a few tablespoons olive oil with an additional teaspoon of cumin and coriander. Mash a cup of cooked beans into onions and garlic. Blend back into the soup. Serve by placing a peeled hard-boiled egg into each bowl. Pour in soup and garnish with fresh coriander leaves.

FAVA BEAN PURÉE

Make recipe for either fresh or dried Fava Bean Soup. Mash all the beans and moisten to consistency of mashed potatoes. Season with additional amounts of cumin, coriander, and garlic if desired. The purée makes an unusual dip with pita and fresh vegetables.

Three Bean Soup

This recipe specifies soaking and cooking times for favas, chickpeas, and lentils, the beans of the bible.

1 large onion or leek, chopped
1 clove garlic, mashed
2 celery stalks with leaves, chopped
1 tablespoon olive oil
$\frac{1}{2}$ teaspoon cumin
$\frac{1}{2}$ teaspoon coriander
Bay leaf
$\frac{1}{2}$ teaspoon thyme

1 handful parsley, chopped
$\frac{1}{2}$ cup dry fava beans, soaked in water for 48 hours
$\frac{1}{4}$ cup dry chickpeas, soaked in water for 24 hours
6 cups water
$\frac{1}{4}$ cup dry lentils
$\frac{1}{4}$ cup pearl barley
Salt and pepper to taste

In a large soup pot, sauté onions, garlic, and celery in olive oil. Add herbs (reserve some parsley for garnish) and spices except salt and continue to sauté for 5 minutes. Add fava beans and chickpeas and water. Cook for one hour. Add barley and lentils and cook for another hour until tender. Garnish with parsley. Salt and pepper to taste before serving. This soup can be served hot or cold. It keeps well and can be frozen.

Fresh Fava Beans With Ground Lamb (Mefarka)

Mefarka is a Middle Eastern chili—chopped meat, beans, and spices, including cumin (a Holy Land native also popular with Mexican cooks).

3 pounds fresh unshelled
   fava beans or 1 pound
   frozen
2 quarts water
2 tablespoons olive oil
1 pound ground lamb
1 teaspoon dried thyme or
   2 teaspoons fresh
$\frac{1}{2}$ teaspoon cumin

$\frac{1}{2}$ teaspoon coriander
$\frac{1}{2}$ teaspoon cinnamon
$\frac{1}{2}$ teaspoon dried mint or
   1 teaspoon fresh
2 eggs, beaten
2 teaspoons salt
1 tablespoon black cumin
   seed (optional)

Shell fresh fava beans. In a large pot with a vented lid, simmer the fresh or frozen fava beans in $\frac{1}{2}$ cup water and 2 tablespoons olive oil for 30 minutes to an hour or until tender. Add more water as it evaporates, but keep water level low. In a large skillet, boil the ground lamb in 1 cup water for 5 minutes. Pour off this water, which will contain much of the excess fat. Return skillet to the heat and let lamb begin to fry in the remaining fat. Stir in the spices and herbs except for the black cumin. Continue frying for about 10 minutes until texture is dry. Mash cooked fava beans into cooked lamb. Add beaten eggs and stir until eggs are set. Add salt and garnish with black cumin seed. Serve with a salad of orange sections and fresh mint leaves, olives, cheese and Whole Wheat Sourdough Bread.

Classic Sabbath Casserole

Remember the Sabbath day to keep it holy. Six days you shall labor and do all your work, but the seventh day is the Sabbath of the Lord thy God. In it you shall do no work: you, nor your son, nor your daughter, nor your manservant, nor your cattle, nor your stranger who is within your gates. Exodus 20:8–10

The Fourth Commandment forbade all labor on the Sabbath, including cooking and housework. Before sundown on the Sabbath, casseroles were placed in the embers of the Sabbath fire to bake overnight, providing a hearty one-dish meal for the day of rest. Records of this type of cooking date as far back as the Second Temple, about the time of Jesus.

2 cups dried hulled fava beans or other dry white beans

3 onions, diced

3 pounds brisket or lamb shanks

3 tablespoons olive oil

2 teaspoons ground cumin

2 teaspoons ground coriander

2 cloves garlic, crushed

2 teaspoons salt

1 cup pearl barley

2 tablespoons whole wheat flour

1 teaspoon capers

1 tablespoon olives, chopped

2 tablespoon raisins

6 cups boiling water (approximately)

Soak the fava beans for 1 to 2 days. Other dry white beans need only be soaked overnight. In a Dutch oven, brown the onions and meat in olive oil. Sprinkle on the spices and salt, stirring as the onions brown. Stir in all other ingredients except the water. Pour in enough boiling water to rise an inch above mixture. Cover tightly with lid. Bake for 24 hours in an oven at 250°F or 4 to 5 hours at 350°F. Serve with fresh fruit, a salad, and Pistachio Almond Cookies.

Lentil Pancakes

. . . there was a piece of ground full of lentils.   2 Samuel 23:11

This ancient cooking method of drying and grinding beans into flour works with chickpeas and fava beans also.

1 cup lentils	**¼ cup honey**
3 eggs	**Olive or sesame oil**

Spread lentils on an ungreased pie plate or baking sheet and roast in a moderate (300°F) oven for 20 minutes. Lentils should be completely dried out and easy to grind. Put lentils through a nut or coffee grinder, or mortar and pestle until they are powdered into the texture of flour. Set aside.

In a large bowl, beat the eggs. Add the honey. Mix well and add the ground lentils, blending thoroughly into a batter. Oil a griddle or large pan and cook like pancakes. Serve with Tabbouleh Salad, steamed vegetables, or as a sweet with grape honey or date syrup.

BREAD

✠ ✠ ✠ ✠

Bread is mentioned hundreds of times in the Bible, more times than any other food. The word can refer generally to all food, but most often it means the loaves, cakes, and biscuits we commonly recognize as bread. The Bible records many instances of brethren eating bread together, of a stranger being given bread, and of God providing bread to his people. Jesus describes himself as the Bread of Life (John 6:35).

The first breads of the Bible were unleavened. Similar to soft tortillas when hot, they cooled into crackers and crisp breads. Barley, the most plentiful grain of the Holy Land, was the chief flour. Barley produces more grain per acre and requires less water than wheat. However, it lacks the abundant gluten of wheat. Gluten is a protein which allows for the enzymatic action of yeast. Two primitive wheats, emmer and einkorn, grew alongside barley. Many centuries of refinement in Egypt, Mesopotamia, and Rome were necessary to produce the bread wheats we know today.

Barley cakes are specifically mentioned in the Scriptures as an integral part of the diet of the early Hebrews. The Feast of Unleavened Bread was an ancient barley harvest festival which became part of Passover (Leviticus 23:6). In Judges 7:13, Gideon dreams of a barley cake that rolls through the camp of a besieging enemy, knocking down their tents. If you ever have day-old leftovers of unleavened barley cake, this story will seem less fantastic. Barley loaves were distributed by Jesus and the Disciples (John 6:9–13), the original loaves and fishes.

The yearly flooding of the Nile Valley enabled the regular cultivation of wheat. The baking skills of the early Hebrews were enlarged by their sojourn in Egypt, for the Egyptians developed the technology of natural yeasts and its applications in leavening bread and brewing beer. A mixture of wheat flour and water left to sit in a warm place for a few days will ferment, developing the yeasts that cause bread dough to rise. We are familiar with this process in the making of sourdough bread. Warmth and timing are key factors in its success. Natural leavening, or sourdough starter, traps air within the bread, producing a lighter, larger-volume loaf than one made with the same amount of unleavened flour.

Ancient papyri record over thirty different Egyptian breads. Stone carvings from the Egyptian tombs show loaves shaped to look like cows and birds, and coiled into spiral snakes. Triangular breads were stacked against each other on racks and small rolls were offered to the gods, two hundred at a time.

The Hebrews did not entirely trust this process of leavening learned from their Egyptian taskmasters (Exodus 12:15). They considered the heaviness of unleavened bread a sign of its purity and wholesomeness; the lightness of leavened bread was a trickery, a sign of corruption. This concept endured in the early Christian writings (1 Corinthians 5:7, and Matthew 16:6).

Unleavened breads of wheat and barley, sometimes referred to as showbreads in the Bible, remained important for ceremonial offerings. Most Bible readers are familiar with the story of the Hebrews fleeing Egypt in such haste that their bread could not be leavened (Exodus 12:34). The matzah of Passover commemorates this liberation. The ancient preference for unleavened bread was recorded in stone on the Roman arch, built after the conquest of the Holy Land, which depicted captive Hebrews forced to present their showbread as a tribute to the emperor. The communion wafer is a latter-day descendant of the traditional unleavened breads.

The first baking ovens were portable, clay cylinders, much like oversized jars. A fire was made in the bottom of the oven. When it had burned down, the ashes were swept out and the bread placed on the cylinder walls to bake by the retained heat. This method was a substantial improvement over the one which preceded it, the baking of bread on flat stones at the edge of the fires. Baking is one culinary technology particularly amenable to specialization, and large-scale baking became necessary in Egypt to feed the laborers of long-term projects such as the building of pyramids. In Mesopotamia, bakeries were connected to the temples, physically and psychologically. The ancient Hebrew state also developed large-scale, professional bakeries. The production of the Sabbath bread was taken over by one family in Jerusalem.

Sarah's Bread

Abraham hastened into the tent unto Sarah and said, "Quickly, make ready three measures of fine flour; knead it and make cakes." Genesis 18:6

This occasion of hospitality is the first biblical reference to baking. Fine flour means wheat flour, not the more common barley, and three measures is approximately twenty-eight cups. Hence, Abraham directs that the finest provisions of the household be offered to his guests. The Patriarchial family included numerous servants, retainers, relatives, and their children. As there were only three guests, the lavish amount of flour suggests that the entire household would share in the meal.

$3\frac{1}{2}$ cups whole wheat flour
  plus extra for flouring
  boards
1 teaspoon salt

$\frac{3}{4}$ cup lukewarm water
Sesame or vegetable oil

Sift together flour and salt. Add the water and mix with a wooden spoon into a smooth paste. Turn onto a floured board and knead at least 10 minutes. Put dough in a bowl and cover with a damp cloth. Let sit in a warm place for 1 to 3 hours. Divide the dough into eight pieces and form into balls. On the floured board, roll each piece into a flat circle about 6 inches across. Cover these pieces with the damp cloth and let sit for 30 minutes. Cook each bread individually in a lightly oiled frying pan or bake several pieces at 500°F until the edges curl up. The adventurous may use large flat stones or oiled, unglazed tiles at the side of a fireplace or outdoor barbecue grill. The object here is to get the bread as close to the heat as possible without burning it in the fire.

Matzah, the Unleavened Bread

They baked unleavened cakes of the dough which they brought
out of Egypt; for it was not leavened, because they were driven
out of Egypt and could not wait . . .   Exodus 12:39

Unleavened bread is considered the "bread of affliction"
and is the only bread permitted to Jews during the week of
Passover.* It is easy to make, and many people find it extremely tasty.

2 cups whole wheat flour or $\frac{3}{4}$ cup water
1 cup whole wheat flour
  and 1 cup barley flour

Combine flour and water thoroughly with wooden spoon.
Dust the top of this mixture with a small amount of flour.
Flour hands and knead the dough lightly for 3 minutes. Divide into 6 to 8 balls, rounding them with floured hands. Oil
a cookie sheet or use a heavy one that does not require oiling. Place balls on cookie sheet. Press down each ball with
hands to make a flat cracker about 5 inches in diameter. Prick
with a fork, to prevent swelling. Bake for 10 minutes in a hot
preheated oven (500°F). Remove matzahs and serve soon if
they are to be eaten soft. Otherwise, turn off the oven and
leave the matzahs in until the oven is cool. They will now
have the consistency of crisp bread and can be stored in air-
tight canisters for long periods. Serve with soups and cheese
spreads.

*To qualify for Passover use today, no more than 17 minutes may elapse from the
time the flour is moistened, the matzah mixed, kneaded, and placed in the oven.

Barley Cakes

And thou shalt eat it as barley cakes . . .   Ezekiel 4:12

$1\frac{1}{2}$ cups hot milk
$\frac{1}{4}$ teaspoon salt
3 tablespoons honey

3 cups barley flour
$\frac{3}{4}$ cup raisins
Oil for frying

Combine all ingredients and shape into balls. Flatten into rounds. Fry in hot oil 5 minutes on each side or bake 20 to 25 minutes in a preheated oven at 400°F. Serve with Ur, Green Butter Herb Cheese.

Beer Bread

This quickly prepared bread is leavened through the action of the yeasts common to both beer brewing and bread baking, two culinary arts widely practiced in Mesopotamia and Egypt.

3 cups whole wheat flour
1 twelve-ounce bottle beer
1 tablespoon honey
$1\frac{1}{2}$ teaspoons salt

3 tablespoons olive or other
    vegetable oil (optional)
$\frac{1}{2}$ cup scallions, chopped
    (optional)

Combine flour, beer, honey, and salt. Knead for 10 minutes or until the dough feels resilient. Place in a bowl and cover with a damp dish towel and let rise for at least one hour. Continue in one of the following ways:

PLAIN

Divide dough into 4 pieces. Shape into balls. Flatten with hand or a rolling pin until $\frac{1}{2}$ inch thick. Place on baking sheet and bake for 45 minutes at 350°F.

SCALLION

Divide into 8 pieces. Shape into small balls and roll out into the thickness of pie crust. Brush with oil and sprinkle with the scallions. Roll up the long way. Pinch ends, pull out, and make into a ball. Flatten to about $\frac{1}{4}$ inch. Fry in oil, turning until brown on both sides.

Serve warm. May be reheated.

Preparing Naturally Leavened Bread (Sourdough)

Sourdough baking requires three stages of leavening flour and water by natural yeasts. These stages are the starter, the sponge, and the dough. A few days are needed to swing into full production, but once organized, one can easily turn out delicious breads and cakes.

The first step is to make the *starter*. Combine 2 cups of flour and 2 cups of water in a glass or ceramic bowl with a wooden spoon. Let sit uncovered for 2 to 5 days in a warm place, stirring occasionally. The mixture needs contact with the air so that invisible airborne yeasts can enter it. The yeasts cause the release of gases, changing the volume and texture of the mixture. When ready, the flour and water will have a clean, yeasty smell and small bubbles, and will be stickier than the original paste. This is sourdough starter and it is ready to leaven breads and cakes. Should contamination occur, off-colors like orange or blue will appear and a disagreeable odor will be exuded. Discard, scald bowl, and start again.

The second step is to make the *sponge*. Add 2 cups of whole wheat flour and 2 cups of warm water to the starter. (These amounts may be increased in specific recipes). Blend well. Cover and let sit for 8 to 10 hours or overnight in a warm spot. The resulting sponge will double in volume and seem sticky like the starter. Take 1 cup of sponge and keep aside in a cool place. After a day or two, the reserved sponge becomes the starter for the next baking.

The third step is to make the *dough*. Add 3 cups of flour and 1 to 2 cups of water to the sponge along with the eggs, milk, honey, or oil called for in a specific recipe. Blend these ingredients and turn onto a floured board for kneading. Knead for a minimum of 10 minutes, then return dough to bowl. Cover and let sit in a warm place for 2 to 4 hours. The dough will double in volume. This is called rising or proofing. After the first rising, the leavened dough is turned back onto a floured board and shaped into loaves, rolls, and cakes. The shaped loaves are left to rise for 1 to 2 hours. A loaf of sourdough bread is generally baked for an hour at 350°F. Higher temperatures produce a chewier crust.

The warmth of your kitchen will determine the exact times necessary to produce sourdough starter, sponge, and dough. Times may vary as much as twenty-four hours, so the above directions are meant only as a general guide. You may prefer your sourdough quite sour and wish to allow extra time in each phase of starter, sponge, and dough.

Starter should never be stored in a tightly closed container, as the gases can build up and cause a small explosion. Starter may be kept in the refrigerator, but will require a few wake-up hours at room temperature before use. If the original starter is not regularly used to make sponge, it will become very sour and should be refreshed weekly with 1 cup flour and 1 cup warm water.

The ancient storage method for starter was to dry it into a hard nugget, and this is still the best way if starter will not be used for a few weeks. Let a cup of sponge dry at room temperature (sunlight speeds the process) into a hard, dry lump. Dried starter is reconstituted by soaking in water for 3 to 12 hours: Keep the dry lump underwater by inverting a dish on top of the container in which it is soaking.

The principles of sourdough baking are those used in the production of any fermented product. Yogurt, wine, and penicillin are made the same way. The natural, healthy yeast is nurtured through warmth, regulation, and adequate food supply. Extremes in temperature such as freezing and baking retard and ultimately kill the yeasts. This is why only warm water is added to the different phases and why baking ingredients should be at room temperature. The yeasts of sourdough baking are among nature's most resilient fungi. Starters have been known to be in continuous use for eighty years.

Whole Wheat Sourdough Bread

Our familiar whole wheat loaf was a luxury to the working people of the Bible. They generally mixed the cheaper barley and wheat flour together, as in the variation on page 134 This master recipe can be used for loaves, flat breads, pitas, and rolls.

The evening before baking, prepare the sponge:

1 cup sourdough starter   **2 cups warm water**
2 cups whole wheat flour

Mix together in a wooden or plastic bowl (avoid metal) and let sit overnight in a warm place. Remove one cup of sponge and set aside to be used as starter in the future. The next day, prepare the dough as follows:

6 cups whole wheat flour   **2 tablespoons honey**
  plus one cup for kneading   **2 tablespoons vegetable oil**
2 cups warm water   **Sesame seed or black cumin**
2 teaspoons salt

Combine flour, water, salt, and honey with sponge into a smooth dough and turn onto a floured board. Knead with floured hands for 10 minutes or 300 times, adding more flour if necessary to keep dough stiff and surfaces floured. If you are kneading with a food processor use only $5\frac{1}{2}$ cups flour. Process for 30 seconds until a ball of dough forms. Place kneaded dough in bowl, brush top with vegetable oil, and cover. Allow to rise for 3 hours in a warm place.

Reknead briefly and shape into 2 loaves. Let sit in a warm place for another 2 hours. Slit the tops, so loaves will not crack while baking. Brush tops with water occasionally to retain moisture. Preheat oven to 350°F and bake about one hour. Test for doneness by inserting a knife. If bread is done, the knife will come out dry. If bread is undercooked, check after 10 minutes. Allow the bread to sit at least 10 minutes before serving or slicing.

SHAPED ROLLS

After allowing dough to rise for 3 hours, reknead briefly and divide into 16 pieces. Make snakes or spirals by rolling dough with hands into thin ropes on a floured surface. Braid, coil, or attach ends for circlets. Shape into triangles. Place on a baking sheet and let rise for an hour. Sprinkle with sesame seed or black cumin if desired. Preheat oven to 450°F. Bake 10 to 15 minutes.

PITAS OR POCKET BREADS

Divide dough into 16 small balls. Shape each piece into a ball on a floured surface or between palms. Cover to keep off drafts and let sit in warm place for 10 to 20 minutes. Preheat oven to 450°F. Roll out with a rolling pin on a floured surface, turning pin to make a circle between $\frac{1}{8}$ and $\frac{1}{4}$ inch thick. The rounds must be evenly flat to make a pocket. Place on unoiled baking sheets and bake 10 minutes.

BREAD BAKED IN A CLAY POT

In ancient times, a wet clay pot was started at the edge of the fire and moved into the hot coals gradually, so that the clay would not break. A small clay pot with a cover, approximately $6'' \times 9''$, works well for a single loaf of bread. Cut the above recipe by one-half. Soak the bottom section of the pot in water for 15 minutes before shaping the dough and putting it into the soaked pot for the last rising. Do not grease the pot. Fifteen minutes before baking, soak the clay top in water. Cover the bread and put in a cold oven which you turn immediately to 475°F. Bake for 45 minutes, taking the cover off for the last ten minutes to brown the top. Test by inserting a knife. If it comes out dry, bread is done.

BARLEY WHEAT SOURDOUGH BREAD

Then a man came from Baal Shalisha, and brought the man of God bread of the firstfruits, twenty loaves of barley bread and newly ripened grain in his knapsack. And he said, "Give it to the people, that they may eat."   2 Kings 4:42

Prepare Whole Wheat Sourdough Bread, substituting for the 6 cups of whole wheat flour in the dough:

2 cups barley flour   1 extra cup either flour for
4 cups whole wheat flour   kneading

To serve a multitude with a barley loaf and two small fishes, as in John 6:8–11, make anchovy toast.

ANCHOVY TOAST

1 loaf Barley Wheat $\frac{1}{4}$ cup olive oil
  Sourdough Bread   1 tablespoon vinegar
4 ounces anchovies   1 tablespoon capers
5 cloves garlic

Slice the bread and set aside. Mash anchovies and garlic into a paste. Slowly add the oil, stirring to blend, then the vinegar. Spread sparingly on slices of bread. Place on cookie sheet. Toast in the oven or under the broiler until golden. Sprinkle on capers. Serve immediately.

DATE NUT BREAD

Jericho, famous for its dates, was called the city of palms, in reference to its date trees. This ancient-style recipe is naturally rich and moist and needs no milk or eggs.

2 cups naturally leavened
  sponge (see page 130)
4 cups whole wheat flour
2 cups warm water
2 cups dried dates, chopped

1 teaspoon salt
2 tablespoons date syrup or
  honey
4 tablespoons vegetable oil
½ to 1 cup chopped walnuts

To the naturally leavened sponge add the rest of the ingredients and mix well. Turn the dough onto a floured board. Knead for 10 minutes. Add more flour and water as necessary to achieve the right texture (on the dry side). Divide into loaves and place on oiled baking pans. Place the loaves in a warm spot, gently covered. Allow to rise for 2 to 3 hours. Slit the tops with a knife and brush the loaves with water. Bake in a moderately hot oven (375°F) for an hour. Brush the tops with water once or twice while baking to conserve moisture. Cool in the pan for 10 minutes before removing.

As with many sourdough breads, this one is even better a day or two after baking. Date nut bread, a mild white cheese, olives, and mint tea make a perfect light lunch.

Sourdough Fig Roll

*And they gave him a piece of a cake of figs and two clusters of
raisins. So when he had eaten, his strength came back to
him . . .*   1 Samuel 30:11–12

2 cups warm water
2 cups sponge (see page 130)
2 cups whole wheat flour
    plus extra for kneading
1 teaspoon salt
3 tablespoons honey

1 teaspoon cinnamon
3 tablespoons vegetable oil
1 cup fig preserves
¼ cup sesame seed
    (optional)

Combine sponge and warm water. Add flour, salt, honey,
cinnamon, and oil. Knead the dough for 10 minutes to a
smooth, dry texture on a floured board. Add small amounts
of flour or water if necessary. With a floured rolling pin, roll
dough into a square or rectangle about ½ inch thick. Spread
the fig preserves over the rolled dough and sprinkle on the
sesame seed. Roll up into a cylinder. Slit the top with a knife,
place in a greased baking pan, and let sit for 1 to 3 hours,
depending on the warmth of the kitchen. Brush tops with
water during the rising and baking. Bake in a preheated oven
at 350°F for one hour.

For individual fig cakes: When cylindrical loaf has been
rolled up, cut into thick slices. Lay these slices on greased
baking sheet and let rise for an hour. Bake the fig cakes for
20 minutes in an oven preheated to 350°F.

Sabbath Bread or Challah

For the Sabbath, each family prepares two loaves of bread to recall the double portion of Sabbath manna provided by God in the desert (Exodus 16:22). The preparation of Sabbath bread became quite elaborate in ancient Jerusalem and was eventually handled by professional bakers.

5 eggs
1 tablespoon salt
½ cup honey
8 cups whole wheat flour
   plus 1 cup for kneading
½ cup water

½ cup vegetable oil
3 cups sponge (see page
   130)
2 tablespoons toasted sesame seed (optional)

Have ingredients at room temperature. In a large bowl, beat 4 eggs, salt, honey, flour, water, and oil. Blend thoroughly. Add the sponge. Turn onto a floured board and knead for 10 minutes. Place dough in a bowl, cover, and let rise in a warm place for 3 to 5 hours.

Turn back on floured board and divide dough into 2 pieces. Divide each piece into thirds and roll the 6 pieces into ropes about 12 inches long. Braid pieces together into a loaf, pushing the ends together. Place on an oiled baking sheet and slit the top of each section.

Let rise again in a warm place for about 2 hours. Preheat the oven to 350°F. Beat remaining egg and brush tops. Sprinkle with sesame seed. Bake 30 to 40 minutes. Turn oven off and leave loaves in an additional 5 minutes. Loaves should shake free of pans. Cool on racks. Challah can be frozen.

Braids may be curled into a circle. Four braids may be used instead of three. The fourth braid is narrower than the other three and placed atop the loaf.

Apricot Raisin Sourdough Bread

*When David was a little past the top of the mountain, there was
Ziba, the servant of Mephibosheth, who met him with a couple of
saddled donkeys, and on them two hundred loaves of bread,
one hundred clusters of raisins, one hundred summer fruits,
and a skin of wine.*   2 Samuel 16:1

1 cup sponge (see page 130)

1 cup applesauce

2 cups whole wheat flour plus extra for kneading

1 teaspoon salt

2 tablespoons honey, barley malt, or date syrup

1½ tablespoons vegetable oil

2 teaspoons cinnamon

½ cup fresh or dried apricots, chopped, and soaked in apricot nectar to cover

½ cup raisins, soaked in apple juice to cover

Have all ingredients at room temperature. Combine and
turn mixture onto floured board for kneading. Knead at least
10 minutes. Form a loaf, slit the top, and brush with water.
Allow to sit for at least 2 hours in a warm place. If loaf loses
its shape from overproofing, simply reknead and reshape.
Brush top of loaf with water to conserve moisture. Brush again
while baking. Preheat oven to 375°F and bake loaf for one
hour. This bread keeps well and is delightful for sandwiches
or cinnamon toast, or spread with Apricot Curd.

Onion Board

This delicious bread was traditionally served at, but was not restricted to, the feast held after circumcision of an infant male, which was required by the covenant between God and Abraham (Genesis 17:10).

1 cup sponge (see page 130)
4 to 5 cups whole wheat flour
1 cup warm water
1 tablespoon honey
3 tablespoons vegetable oil

2 eggs
4 cups onion, chopped
1 tablespoon vegetable oil
Salt and pepper to taste
1 tablespoon poppy seed (optional)

Combine first six ingredients into a smooth dough. Knead the dough on a floured surface. Put dough back in bowl, cover, and place in warm spot for 2 hours to rise, until doubled in size.

Meanwhile, sauté onions in vegetable oil until golden. Remove from heat and add salt, pepper, and poppy seeds.

After dough rises, divide into 4 parts. On a floured surface, roll each of the 4 parts into a flat oblong. Sprinkle with sautéed onion mixture. Puncture boards with a fork in several places. Bake on an oiled cookie sheet in an oven preheated to 350°F for 35 to 40 minutes. Crusts should be golden and onions caramel brown. Serve fresh from oven.

Carob Spicery Seed Bread

And they sat down to eat a meal. Then they lifted their eyes and looked and there was a company of Ishmaelites coming from Gilead with their camels, bearing spicery, balm, and myrrh on their way to carry them down to Egypt. Genesis 37:25

3 cups sponge (see page 130)
3 cups whole wheat flour
$\frac{1}{2}$ cup carob flour
2 tablespoons vegetable oil
2 teaspoons cinnamon
4 tablespoons honey or date syrup
1 teaspoon anise seed
1 teaspoon ground black pepper
Pinch of cumin
2 tablespoons toasted sesame seed
1 tablespoon poppy seed
1 cup yogurt
Warm water

Combine all ingredients into a dough. Knead the dough at least 10 minutes. Shape into two loaves and place them on oiled baking pans. Let rise for 3 hours, reshaping if necessary. Carob must be baked at low temperature to prevent burning. Preheat oven to 300°F. Place a pan of warm water in the oven alongside the baking pans. Bake for 2 hours. Let rest in pans 10 minutes before removing.

Sprouted Essene Bread

Moisten your wheat that the angel of water may enter
it . . .   Essene Gospel of Peace

The Essenes were an ascetic community that influenced the early Christian church. They were expert bakers of sprouted breads, a technique that produces a sweet, moist, cakelike bread without honey, eggs, or oil. This recipe was in the manuscripts discovered as the Dead Sea Scrolls.

6 cups hard durum wheat kernels (available in health food stores)
10 cups water

½ cup raisins (optional)
½ cup almonds or walnuts (optional)

Use a large sprouter from a health food store or several large jars and porous covering material for the tops, such as cheesecloth or clean metal screening. Use four 1-quart jars, putting 1½ cups of wheat kernels and 2½ cups of water in each jar. Cover the top with a piece of cloth or screening large enough to overlap the edge by an inch or two. Fasten the top tightly around the neck of each jar with a rubber band, or string, or if using canning jars, the outer canning band without the center disk. Leave kernels in water overnight and drain through the strainer top in the morning.

After 8 hours, rinse the wheat with water and drain immediately without removing the cloth covering. Continue rinsing and draining the sprouts 2 to 3 times a day for the next 2 to 4 days. The sprouts will vary in length. When the sprouts are about as long as the kernel, they are ready to use. Two cups of kernels will expand to about 4½ cups of sprouts.

Use a food processor with metal blade or meat grinder to grind the sprouts into a smooth, sticky mass. Grind 2 cups at one time for about 3 minutes. With a food processor the dough will first become very smooth, then ball up and break apart. Watch carefully. Immediately after it forms a ball, take out of the food processor or grinder and add nuts or raisins as desired. Shape into 2 or more round loaves. Place on a well oiled baking sheet. Cover and let rest for an hour.

Bake for 1½ to 2 hours at 300°F or 3 to 4 hours at 250°F. Some cooks feel that the longer, slower baking temperatures preserve the freshness of the sprouted wheat. Up to an additional 30 minutes of baking time may be needed to brown the crust. This bread keeps well and is better if kept a day or two before serving.

Sprouted Ezekiel Bread

Take for yourself wheat, barley, beans, lentils, millet and spelt and put them into one vessel and make bread of them for yourself.   Ezekiel 4:9

Ezekiel bread is one of the most specific recipes of the Scriptures. Bible readers will notice that it is not intended as a delicacy for a joyous occasion. Rather, it was an emergency survival food to be prepared during the dire straits of the Babylonian conquest. This version uses all Ezekiel's ingredients except spelt, an inferior wheat no longer available. The passage suggests that the bread may have been sprouted.

$\frac{3}{4}$ cup hard winter wheat
   kernels
$\frac{1}{8}$ cup chickpeas
$\frac{1}{8}$ cup lentils

$\frac{1}{4}$ cup millet flour
$\frac{1}{4}$ cup barley flour

Sprout and grind wheat kernels, chickpeas, and lentils, following instructions in the Sprouted Essene Bread recipe. Add the millet and barley flour (millet and barley do not easily sprout). Shape the dough into 5 or 6 individual patties. Put on an oiled baking sheet and bake for 2 hours in an oven preheated to 200°F. Brush tops with water to retain moisture. Turn and bake for another $1\frac{1}{2}$ hours at 250°F. Serve warm.

DAIRY

. . . *curds from the cattle and milk from the flock* . . . Deuteronomy 32:14

So I have come down to deliver them out of the hand of the Egyptians and to bring them up from that land to a good and large land, to a land flowing with milk and honey. Exodus 3:8

While meat was generally reserved for special occasions, dairy products sustained the people of the Bible daily. Milk, like honey, was considered a special food because it was produced by animals solely for the purpose of nourishment. The Bible specifically mentions the milk of cows and sheep (Deuteronomy 32:14), camels (Genesis 32:15), and goats (Proverbs 27:27).

Milk was regarded as a physical and spiritual extension of the mother animal. Ancient Egyptian pictures show a cow weeping as her milk is taken while her thirsty calf looks on. Pagan religions paid homage to the connection of birth, milk, and motherhood through fertility rites in which calves were cooked in their mother's milk. Ceremonies of this nature were forbidden the Hebrews by the injunction "You shall not boil a young kid in its mother's milk" (Exodus 23:19). This regulation is one of the cornerstones of the dietary laws, known as kosher or kasruth. It was interpreted as forbidding any use of meat and dairy products in the same dish or even at the same meal. This separation of meat and dairy meals differentiated the cuisine of the Hebrews from that of traditional Middle Eastern groups.

Fresh milk could not be kept well in the hot climate of the Holy Land. So the principles of fermentation used in wine making and sourdough baking were also applied to the preservation of milk. The result was yogurt and cheese. The Hebrew language of the Bible had three terms for dairy products, which roughly correspond to yogurt, soft cheese, and hard cheese. The original King James Bible translated all these terms as "butter." The New King James Version uses the word "curds," a closer approximation to the actual foods, which were similar to our yogurts and simple white cheeses. Butter was a common food, considered the staple of shepherds, but for cooking, olive oil was preferred.

CHEESES ✠ ✠

Basic Fresh Curd Cheese

In Biblical times every family knew how to make fresh cheese from the surplus milk of the sheep, goats, and cows they kept. As with many ancient technologies, this cheesemaking is neither elaborate nor difficult, but requires organization and patience. Cheesemaking concentrates the milk proteins, leaving a nutritious liquid, whey. One gallon of fresh milk makes a half pound of cheese and several cups of whey. Whey should be treated as a light stock: enriching to soups and stews, sipped plain or lightly flavored, and always refrigerated.

To make most cheese, use sour milk. Fresh unpasteurized milk is soured simply by leaving it out of the refrigerator uncovered, overnight. Standard homogenized, pasteurized milk is soured by the addition of *1 tablespoon vinegar or lemon juice to every 2 cups lukewarm milk.*

Heat the sour milk over low heat until solids separate. The solid mass is called the clabber. Pour this into a strainer or colander lined with a double layer of cheesecloth. Place the colander or strainer over a bowl to catch the whey. Any clean, open-weave, undyed fabric may be substituted for cheesecloth (two layers of wet paper toweling will do in a pinch). Let the cheese drip overnight or at least 6 hours. Form the cheese into small balls and eat plain or seasoned as in the following recipes.

Pressed Coriander Cheese

1 recipe Basic Fresh Curd
  Cheese, using 5 cups milk

2 tablespoons coriander
  leaves, minced

This is a pressed fresh cheese. To the fresh curds add the minced coriander and knead into the cheese. Rewrap cheese in cheesecloth and flatten it with hands to make a patty about 4 inches wide.

Place the wrapped cheese on a strong plate and weigh down with a heavy object, such as a cast-iron pan. Leave the weight on for at least 5 hours. The finished cheese will be a cake about $\frac{1}{2}$ to $\frac{3}{4}$ inch thick. Remove from cheesecloth and serve as is or cut into bite-size pieces. Toasted pita bread and olives are good accompaniments.

Yogurt Cheese

2 cups yogurt $\frac{1}{2}$ teaspoon salt

Salt the yogurt and pour into double cheesecloth, tie up the ends to make a bag, and drain overnight or longer. An alternative method is to line a colander or sieve with cheesecloth and let the yogurt drain into a bowl. The yogurt can be drained for up to 36 hours to make a firmer cheese. Roll cheese into little balls and serve as a finger food. Serve with Beer Bread or Barley Cakes. Yield: 1 cup of cheese.

Cinnamon Cheese

Cinnamon was one of the earliest of traded commodities, caravanned across the desert by camels from the East. It was a favorite scent for perfumes and incense as well as a flavor for food (Exodus 30:23). Cassia, a cinnamonlike bark, mentioned in the Bible was also traded.

$\frac{1}{2}$ pound fresh curd cheese
   at room temperature
   (pot, farmer's, cream, or
   yogurt cheese
2 teaspoons freshly ground
   cinnamon (more if
   desired)

Pinch of salt
1 teaspoon honey or 2
   tablespoons sweet
   grape juice

Combine all ingredients. Store in refrigerator. This dish is excellent on toast. More honey may be added along with nuts and raisins if desired.

Black Cumin Cheese Spread

Does he not sow the black cummin . . . ?   Isaiah 28:25

½ pound fresh curd cheese
   at room temperature
1 teaspoon to 1 tablespoon
   black cumin seed (also
   known as onion seed or
   Nigella sativa)

Salt to taste
1 tablespoon parsley,
   chopped

Combine all ingredients. Let sit overnight in refrigerator. Serve with toast.

Hot Radish Cheese Spread

½ pound fresh curd cheese
   at room temperature
1 tablespoon fresh radish,
   grated *and/or*

½ teaspoon freshly grated
   horseradish (more to
   taste)
Pinch of salt

Combine all ingredients. This is best served fresh. Fresh cucumber sandwiches made with radish cheese spread are excellent with beer.

Fresh Cheese With Seed Relish

. . . parched seeds, honey and curds . . .   2 Samuel 17:29

3 tablespoons fresh squash
   seed
1 tablespoon black or white
   mustard seed
1 teaspoon whole cumin
   seed
1 teaspoon poppy seed

½ pound fresh white cheese
Pinch of clove, cinnamon,
   and coriander
Salt to taste
2 tablespoons honey
   (optional)

In a heavy skillet, roast the squash seed without oil until they begin to crisp. Stir frequently. Add the other seeds and spices; toast lightly until the mustard seed begin to pop. Allow to cool. Sprinkle on top of cheese. Salt to taste. If a sweet version is desired, spoon honey on top of cheese and sprinkle with seed relish. Vary the proportions to taste. Serve with Whole Wheat Sourdough Bread, Lentil Pancakes, or Matzah.

Ur: Green Butter Herb Cheese

For as the churning of milk produces butter . . .   Proverbs 30:33

Butter was sometimes used to pay taxes in the Holy Land. Ur, an herbed mixture of cheese and butter, is an ancient combination that was especially popular with the Babylonians.

1 tablespoon each fresh
   chopped mint, parsley,
   dill, green scallion tops,

½ pound fresh curd cheese:
   cream, farmer's, or
   whipped cottage

coriander leaves, arugola, ¼ pound butter
thyme, and rue Salt to taste

Have cheese and butter at room temperature. Mash herbs, cheese, and butter together. Salt to taste. Let sit for an hour or store overnight in the refrigerator to let flavors mingle. Serve with Matzah, Whole Wheat Sourdough toast, or over warm vegetables. Vary proportions to suit taste.

Basic Goat Cheese Yogurt Spread

¼ cup tart goat cheese at Chopped pistachios
  room temperature Parsley
1 cup yogurt Black cumin
2 tablespoons olive oil
Black olives

Beat cheese and yogurt together into a smooth paste. Vary proportions to suit taste. Moisten with milk or cream if a liquid texture is preferred. Spread a thin layer of the sauce over a few small, flat plates. Drizzle olive oil over the cheese sauce. Garnish with black olives, nuts, parsley, or black cumin. Serve with Sourdough Fig Roll. A bowl of seasoned chickpeas and a salad go nicely with this dish.

Marinated Goat Cheese

Fresh cheese was covered with olive oil and spices to preserve as well as flavor it.

Up to 1½ teaspoons total,
    more to taste:
    bayleaf (crumpled),
    celery seed, whole corian-
    der, cumin seed, thyme,
    dill, fennel seed,
    black pepper

½ to 1 cup olive oil
1 pound fresh goat cheese
Fresh parsley or coriander
    leaves

Select your favorite seasonings and stir them into the olive oil. Let steep for at least an hour. Form cheese into balls or cakes and arrange in one or more suitable containers for marinating. Pour flavored olive oil over cheese and let sit at least one hour before serving. If completely covered by oil, cheese may remain unrefrigerated for several hours. In the refrigerator, olive oil will congeal rather unattractively. Always bring cheese to room temperature before serving. Sprinkle with fresh parsley or coriander leaves. Serve with Matzah, olives, pickles, and beer.

Fresh Cheese With Garlic and Herbs

4 cloves garlic, unpeeled
    (more if desired)
2 tablespoons olive oil
Parsley, thyme, and dill,
    fresh totaling at least a
    tablespoon; if dried, 1
    teaspoon.

½ pound fresh curd cheese
    at room temperature
Salt to taste

Sauté garlic in one tablespoon olive oil, gently, until golden. Let cool. Peel and mash garlic with herbs and additional tablespoon of oil. Mix into cheese. Add salt if necessary. Let sit several hours before serving. Form cheese into balls or small cakes if desired. This garlic cheese and the Marinated Goat Cheese may be used in Hot Goat Cheese With Fresh Herb Salad.

Hot Goat Cheese With Fresh Herb Salad

A selection of bitter herbs for a salad of arugola, endive, watercress, and romaine lettuce.

One cake per serving of Fresh Goat Cheese or Cheese With Garlic and Herbs, about $\frac{1}{2}$ inch thick and $2\frac{1}{2}$ inches wide
$\frac{1}{2}$ cup olive oil

1 tablespoon mustard
1 teaspoon honey
$\frac{1}{8}$ cup wine vinegar
Fresh herbs: coriander leaves, thyme, dill

Marinate the rounds of goat cheese in about $\frac{1}{4}$ cup olive oil for at least 4 hours. Prepare a vinaigrette dressing with the mustard, honey, remaining olive oil, and vinegar. Put rounds of goat cheese on a baking sheet and bake in a preheated hot oven, about 425°F, for 5 to 8 minutes. Cheese should be bubbly and golden. Meanwhile, toss salad with vinaigrette dressing and put into individual bowls. As cheese comes out of the oven, slide one cake onto each salad bowl. Toss hot cheese into the greens. Serve immediately with bread or crackers.

Roman Broccoli Goat Cheese Soup

You shall have enough goat's milk for your food, for the food of your household.   Proverbs 27:27

2 heads broccoli
5 cups water*
$\frac{1}{4}$ pound fresh goat cheese
  (more if desired)
Salt and pepper

Vinegar
Dash of cumin
Chopped scallions
Parsley or coriander

Chop broccoli and boil in the water for 10 minutes. Remove from heat. Add goat cheese to water and broccoli. Put through a blender, mindful that the texture of the vegetables in the soup can be varied from chunky to smooth. The goat cheese should be well creamed into the liquid. Taste. Add salt, pepper, and seasonings as desired. Serve immediately with croutons, bread and butter, and an unusual salad with colors other than green (for example, radishes, oranges, and olives).

*Meat stock can be used in place of water and cream may be added for extra richness.

Goat Cheese and Spinach Soufflé

$\frac{1}{4}$ pound white goat cheese
(such as feta)
$\frac{3}{4}$ pound ricotta or whipped
cottage cheese

4 eggs, beaten
2 pounds cooked spinach or
greens, chopped (frozen
may be used)

Preheat oven to 350°F. Mix all ingredients and pour into an oiled casserole dish. Cover and bake for 45 minutes to an hour or until set. Vary the proportions of goat and ricotta to suit taste. Additional cooked vegetables can be added. Serve hot or cold with Sprouted Essene Bread, Tabbouleh, Fish Cakes, or Three Bean Soup.

YOGURT ✠ ✠

Yogurt, like all thickened milk, was considered to be curds. Warm milk becomes infused with the healthy lactoacidophilus bacteria and thickens. This ancient food has become very familiar in American markets. Good yogurt can be purchased everywhere. However, a delicious, economical yogurt can be produced at home. Powdered milk makes a more consistent product than homogenized milk.

You will need yogurt starter. Yogurt starters can be purchased at health food stores, but we have not found them better than plain commercial yogurt.

Whole Milk Yogurt

1 quart milk   2 tablespoons plain yogurt
                                      or yogurt starter

Heat milk to the boiling point to kill unwanted bacteria, then cool to about 100°F to 110°F (slightly higher than the temperature of the human body; milk will feel warm to the wrist). Add yogurt starter. Mixture must be kept consistently warm to thicken. This can be done in various ways:

1. Put covered bowl in a pan of warm water over a pilot light on the stove or in an oven with a gas pilot light.
2. Put covered bowl on the floor next to a radiator or refrigerator exhaust.
3. Make yogurt mixture in a prewarmed wide-mouth Thermos bottle.
4. Use an electric yogurt maker, following directions.

About 8 hours is necessary for the milk to turn into yogurt.

Powdered Milk Yogurt

Powdered milk makes more consistent yogurt than fresh milk because the antibiotics present in commercial milk today affect the yogurtmaking process.

Dissolve 2 cups powdered milk in 4 cups warm water. Add 2 tablespoons yogurt and follow directions for fresh-milk yogurt.

Each succeeding batch of yogurt is made by using 2 tablespoons from the preceding batch. The texture and taste of yogurt will vary. Thin yogurt is excellent as a drink or can be used as stock in soup. After several batches of yogurt are made, the starter may need to be replaced.

TO STABILIZE YOGURT FOR COOKING
Salted yogurt made of goat's milk may be used directly in cooking. Cow's-milk yogurt will curdle unless pretreated.

Up to 5 cups plain yogurt
1 egg white, beaten

$\frac{3}{4}$ teaspoon salt (use less salt
   for less yogurt)

Put all ingredients in a small saucepan and heat over a low flame, stirring in the same direction, until the mixture begins to boil. Turn down heat and simmer for 5 to 10 minutes or until thick. This yogurt can be used for long cooking without curdling (although an alternative is to stir in the yogurt after food is removed from heat).

Yogurt With Fresh Herbs and Cucumber

Mix fresh yogurt with "every green herb for food" (Genesis 1:30).

2 medium-size cucumbers, thinly sliced (waxed cucumbers must be peeled or well scrubbed)
2 cups fresh plain yogurt
Salt to taste

5 tablespoons or more chopped fresh coriander leaves, parsley, mint, dill, fennel, green onion tops, arugola, very young mustard greens
2 cups buttermilk (optional, see below)

To serve as a soup: Combine all ingredients and let sit for an hour before serving. Chill if desired.

To serve as a sauce or relish: Omit buttermilk and, if desired, cucumber.

Yogurt Sesame Sauce

1 cup plain yogurt
¼ cup sesame paste (tahini)
  (more if desired)
1 to 2 tablespoons vinegar
  or lemon juice

Salt to taste
Sprinkle of herbs: fresh dill,
  coriander leaves, parsley

Combine all ingredients, tasting to adjust proportions. Use low-fat yogurt for an excellent low-cholesterol (though, unfortunately, not low-calorie) sauce for vegetables, sandwiches, and salads.

Yogurt and Mashed Parsnip

Native to the Mediterranean area, the parsnip was a favorite root vegetable in the potato-less world of the Bible, and the unopened flowers of the parsnip were used as an herb. Today, the carrot, first cousin to the parsnip, has eclipsed it in popularity.

1 cup hot boiled parsnips, mashed
1 tablespoon butter (optional)
½ cup plain yogurt
Salt to taste

¼ cup milk or buttermilk
Chopped chives or black cumin seed

Mash the hot parsnips with butter, yogurt, and salt. Thin with milk. Garnish with chopped chives or black cumin seed. Serve immediately or keep warm in a double boiler. Parsnips are deliciously sweet without many calories. Cooked carrots and potatoes can be mashed with the parsnips. Serve with roasted meats.

Yogurt Cumin Seed Sauce

1 cup plain yogurt

1 teaspoon whole cumin seed
Salt to taste

The flavor of this simple, piquant sauce is enhanced by roasting and grinding the cumin. Spread cumin seeds on the bottom of a cast iron skillet. Heat until toasted and fragrant. Crush in a small mill or mortar. Season with salt. This is an excellent sauce for vegetables and meats.

Yogurt Soup With Raisins

2 hard-boiled eggs, chopped
¾ cup raisins, soaked in 2
  cups cold water for 5
  minutes
4 cups yogurt
1 tablespoon vinegar
¾ cup milk
2 cups cucumber, diced

½ cup scallions, chopped
1 teaspoon salt
½ cup blanched slivered
  almonds (optional)
2 tablespoons parsley,
  minced (optional)
2 tablespoons dill, minced
  (optional)

In a large bowl, blend eggs, raisins, cold water, yogurt, vinegar, milk, cucumber, scallions, and salt. Refrigerate for at least 2 hours or heat and serve when thoroughly warmed. Do not boil. Garnish with herbs and nuts as desired. Serve with Matzah, Onion, Olive, and Orange Salad, and Ashurey for dessert.

Chickpea Yogurt Soup
  With Greens

Beets, mustard, and radishes were the popular greens of the Patriarchs. Spinach, introduced by the Persians, was known around the Mediterranean area by the time of Jesus. This recipe is simplified by using pre-spiced chickpea flour. Generally sold as felafel mix, it is moistened and made into fried patties called felafel. It is a popular meat substitute sold in health food stores and some supermarkets.

5 cups water

¾ cup felafel mix* (see below)

1 cup yogurt (sour yogurt may be used)

1 pound of fresh or frozen beet greens or spinach, cooked and drained

2 tablespoons vinegar or lemon juice

1 teaspoon black pepper

2 tablespoons olive oil or untoasted sesame oil

1 teaspoon whole cumin seed

In a bowl, slowly beat ½ cup water into the felafel mix or chickpea flour to maintain a smooth paste. In a separate bowl beat yogurt with remaining water to a frothy cream. Add the yogurt mixture to the chickpeas slowly. Put in a heavy pot and simmer over medium heat. Add greens, pepper, and vinegar or lemon. Cover and simmer for at least one hour, stirring frequently. Add more water if necessary—the mixture will become quite thick. In a small saucepan, heat oil and add cumin seed. Sauté until aroma develops. Add to soup. Serve hot over Basic Barley or Millet or serve as a cold soup.

*If felafel mix is not available, make your own. To powder your own chickpeas read instructions for Lentil Pancakes, page 121.

¾ cup chickpea flour

1 teaspoon ground cumin seed

1 teaspoon ground coriander seed

½ teaspoon turmeric

¼ teaspoon powdered ginger

½ teaspoon garlic powder

3 tablespoons parsley, dill, or mint, chopped

5 tablespoons sautéed or dehyrated onion (optional)

½ teaspoon ground pomegranate seed (optional)

Pinch of saffron

Black pepper

Yogurt Drinks

These drinks are as delicious on a hot day today as they were in biblical times. Dilute yogurt with cool water in a ratio of 1 to 2. Stir or whirl gently through blender with additional flavorings. Serve chilled.

MINT

This ancient combination is good salty or sweet. To a diluted yogurt mixture add 6 sprigs fresh mint, chopped and crushed, and $\frac{1}{2}$ teaspoon salt or 2 tablespoons honey.

COLD CREAMED BEET

Blend one small cooked, shredded beet per cup of diluted yogurt (more if desired). Sweeten with honey if desired. The addition of rose water will make an unusual drink, brilliantly colored and redolent of flowers. Begin with $\frac{1}{4}$ teaspoon of rose water and gradually increase to $\frac{1}{2}$ teaspoon.

CITRON (ORANGE) FLOWER

The flavoring of orange flowers may have preceded the use of the fruit in the Holy Land. Sweeten diluted yogurt with 2 to 3 tablespoons honey and add $\frac{1}{4}$ teaspoon orange flower water (more if desired). Garnish with mint.

POMEGRANATE

Add 3 tablespoons fresh or bottled pomegranate juice to diluted yogurt (more to taste). Sweeten with honey if needed. This drink also has a pale pink color.

DATE

Add 6 fresh or dried and soaked dates (pitted) to diluted

yogurt. Blend and sweeten with additional date syrup if desired.

GRAPE

Sweeten diluted yogurt with fresh grapes or a combination of fresh grapes and grape honey.

CAROB

Mix a tablespoon of carob with a small amount of water. Add ½ tablespoon honey (more to taste) and mix with diluted yogurt. Whirl through a blender.

Persian Yogurt Soup With Meatballs

Queen Esther is reputed to have been so strict in her following of the kosher laws that she ate only seeds and vegetables. However, when she gave a series of banquets to persuade King Ahasuerus to spare her people, she served Middle Eastern classics like this elegant soup.

SOUP

3 cups yogurt
¼ cup cooked millet or uncooked rice
1 egg, beaten
2 tablespoons whole wheat flour
1 teaspoon salt
½ teaspoon pepper

1 teaspoon dried dill or 2 tablespoons fresh
3 cups water
¼ cup parsley, chopped
½ cup cooked chickpeas (canned may be used)
½ cup green onions, chopped

MEATBALLS

½ pound ground beef, lamb, or veal

1 small onion, minced

½ teaspoon salt

½ teaspoon pepper

HOT GARLIC SAUCE (optional)

2 cloves garlic

½ cup melted butter

1 tablespoon dry mint or 2 tablespoons fresh

In a 2-quart saucepan, mix yogurt, millet or rice, egg, flour, and seasonings. Add water and stir. Simmer over a low flame, stirring occasionally, for a half hour. To make meatballs, mix meat, onion, salt, and pepper together in a bowl. Shape into small balls, rolling them between the palms of the hands. When the soup has thickened slightly, add parsley, chickpeas, green onion, and meatballs. Simmer an additional 20 minutes, stirring occasionally. To prepare the garlic sauce, chop the garlic cloves and sauté briefly in melted butter. Add mint and stir well. At the table, put a spoonful of sauce in each serving of soup. Serve with Shaped Rolls and Haroseth.

DESSERTS

✤ ✤ ✤ ✤

F ruits, nuts, and baked goods were the desserts of the ancient world. Dried fruit and nuts were winter staples, often crushed together into sweetmeats or stuffed into pastries. The royal kitchens could prepare elaborate desserts—intricately shaped cakes, rich puddings, and even fruit sherbets with carefully transported mountain snow to refresh the palate. Confectioners sold individual sweetmeats in the bazaars and markets, just as today's shoppers are lured by a variety of sweet snacks.

The favorite sweetener of the ancient world was honey. But apiculture came late to the Holy Land, and for centuries only wild honey was available. As the Bible notes, finding a hive of bees with its cache of honey was looked upon as a fortunate event, if not a gift from God. Honey was considered a precious food of exceptional purity and nutritional and medicinal value. The Hebrews were impressed by the fact that honey was produced by animals as food for themselves. They were forbidden to burn honey on the altar of God (Leviticus 2:11).

Honey figures in the stories of several biblical heroes. Moses sang of honey found between rock crevices in the desert, a favorite nesting place for Sinai bees to this day (Deuteronomy 32:13). Samson found a hive of bees nesting in a slain lion and fashioned a riddle for the Philistines from this unusual occurrence (Judges 14:12–19). Jonathan ate honey dripping onto the ground in the forest and was immediately refreshed, though trouble ensued (1 Samuel 14:24–29).

As might be expected, random finds of wild honey could hardly satisfy the sweet tooth of this sugarless world. Dates, grapes, carob, and other fruits were boiled to make thick syrups that are excellent and unusual sweeteners. Sweet wines of raisins, dates, figs, and grapes were also used for flavoring. A variety of sweet substances were collected from insects other than bees. The liquid honeydew secretions of insects such as the cicada condense rapidly in the sub-Sahara heat of the Holy Land, leaving a sweet granular residue. Scholars suggest that this edible substance, called manna today, fits the description of the famous manna of Exodus, chapter 16.

The Bible twice mentions sweet cane (Isaiah 43:24 and Jeremiah 6:20), which may be references to papyrus from which a sweet sap was extracted, as molasses is from sugar cane. By the time of Jesus, small quantities of sugar, called reed honey, were imported from India. Sugar was considered inferior in all aspects to bee honey, though possessed of some medicinal qualities such as aiding in digestion. The Roman cookbooks of Apicius do not include sugar, known also as Indian salt and Asian honey, among its many ingredient lists.

Ancient people were well-informed consumers of the different flavors and grades of honey. Rare varieties were imported from throughout the known world, with thyme honey especially prized. Guests were honored with sweet foods prepared with fine honeys; the finer the honey, the greater the honor. In addition, honey was used by the early Christian church in baptismal ceremonies.

As beekeeping methods spread, primarily through the Greeks, honey became more widely available. The status of honeyed foods declined, and conspicuous consumption of sweetened foods became associated with overindulgence.

The desserts that follow use honey or fruit sweeteners of grape, date, or carob. Dried fruits and nuts add texture, flavor, and richness.

Fig Pastries

Then Abigail made haste and took . . . two hundred cakes of figs . . .   1 Samuel 25:18

PASTRY

$\frac{3}{4}$ cup unsalted butter
$4\frac{1}{2}$ cups whole wheat pastry flour
1 large egg

2 cups honey
$3\frac{1}{2}$ cups milk

FILLING

1 pound dried figs, chopped
$1\frac{1}{2}$ cups water
$\frac{1}{2}$ cup honey
$\frac{1}{2}$ teaspoon cinnamon

1 tablespoon vinegar or lemon juice

1 egg beaten with 1 tablespoon water

To prepare filling, boil the figs in water for 15 minutes in a saucepan. Add honey and cinnamon and continue to boil for 30 minutes more, stirring frequently until mixture has thickened. Add vinegar or lemon juice. Let mixture cool in saucepan.

To prepare pastry, cream butter and flour in a bowl. Beat in the egg. Add the honey and milk. Form the dough into a large ball. Dust the ball with flour and wrap in a damp cloth. Chill for at least an hour, overnight if possible.

Preheat oven to 375°F. Cut dough into 4 pieces. Cover pieces with damp cloth. On a floured board roll out one piece and cut into 8 or more squares. Place a tablespoon of filling on each square and brush edges with egg mixture. Fold into a triangle, pinching edges together. Place on an oiled baking sheet. Prick tops with fork and brush with beaten egg. Bake for 20 minutes. Serve with Yogurt With Fresh Herbs and Cucumber for an excellent tea or other light meal.

Fig Cake

And they gave him a piece of a cake of figs . . .   1 Samuel 30:12

1 cup butter
½ cup honey
3 cups fig preserves (Apricot preserves may be substituted)
5 egg yolks, beaten
3 cups whole wheat pastry flour

1 cup sour milk, yogurt, or buttermilk
1 cup walnuts, grated
1 cup raisins
1½ tablespoons cinnamon
5 egg whites, stiffly beaten

Cream butter and honey, add figs and egg yolks, and beat until smooth. Add flour and milk alternately. Add nuts, raisins, and cinnamon. Fold in egg whites. Pour into well-oiled 10 inch springform cake pan and bake in oven at 350°F for 1 hour and thirty minutes. Test to make sure cake is done: a knife inserted in the center should come out clean. Serve with Honey Sauce if desired.

Raisin Cake

. . . sustain me with cakes of raisins . . .   Song of Solomon 2:5

4 eggs
$\frac{1}{2}$ cup honey
$\frac{1}{2}$ cup whole wheat pastry
   flour
$\frac{1}{2}$ teaspoon salt

$2\frac{1}{2}$ cups raisins, chopped
   (dates or figs may be substituted)
1 cup almonds
Whipped cream

Preheat oven to 350°F. In a large bowl, beat eggs until fluffy. Gradually beat in honey, flour, salt, raisins, and nuts. Pour batter into oiled 9×9-inch pan. Bake for 30 to 40 minutes. Serve warm with whipped cream.

High-Fiber Fig Cake

The fig is not generally an orchard tree. It grows singly or adjacent to the pomegranate tree in the Holy Land. Simple, nutritious combinations such as this one sustained biblical people through the winter.

1 cup boiling water
1 cup bulghar wheat
1 cup figs., chopped (raisins
   or dates may be substituted)

$\frac{1}{4}$ teaspoon salt

In a large bowl pour boiling water over bulghar wheat. Soak wheat for an hour and drain. Add chopped fruit and salt. Put mixture through a food processor or grinder. Form into small balls or patties. If serving hot is desired, shape mixture into a loaf and bake for 30 minutes at 350°F in an oiled loaf pan. This dish can also be served as a breakfast cereal.

Honey Cakes

The Bible tells of David's triumphant entry into Jerusalem with the ark (2 Samuel 6:13–21). The festivities included dancing and serving honey cakes to all the citizens. This is the legendary origin of the serving of honey cakes for all occasions of great rejoicing, especially weddings.

½ cup melted butter or almond oil
1 cup honey
3 eggs
4 cups whole wheat pastry
 flour

1 teaspoon cinnamon
¼ teaspoon salt
½ cup milk

In a large bowl, cream butter or oil and honey. Add eggs. Sift dry ingredients together and add to creamed mixture alternately with milk. Pour batter into 2 oiled 9-inch cake pans. Bake for 35 minutes in oven preheated to 350°F. Top with cream cheese or honey sauce.

Honey Wine Cake

This is an especially light and elegant version of the festive honey cake.

5 egg yolks
½ cup honey
1 tablespoon orange peel,
 grated
1 cup whole wheat pastry
 flour

½ teaspoon salt
½ cup sweet white wine
½ cup plus 2 tablespoons
 olive oil
7 egg whites

Preheat oven to 375°F. In a small bowl, whisk egg yolks with honey for 5 minutes. Add orange peel.

In a large bowl, sift pastry flour with salt. Gradually stir in egg and honey. Follow with wine and olive oil, stirring constantly as small amounts are added.

Beat the egg whites until stiff and fold into batter. Line the bottom of an 8-inch spring-form pan with oiled parchment or thick brown paper (cut from a brown paper bag if necessary). Oil the pan and paper well. Pour in batter and bake for 20 minutes. Turn oven off and let cake sit for 10 minutes. It will deflate.

Remove cake from oven. Turn over and detach from spring pan carefully. Serve with wine. Store in refrigerator.

Honey Sauce

1½ cups honey   1 egg white
⅛ teaspoon salt

Cook honey and salt to 245°F or until it spins a thread and forms a firm ball when dropped into cold water. Beat egg white. Pour syrup in thin stream over beaten egg white. Continue beating until sauce stands in peaks.

Fennel Seed Cake

*Also take with you . . . some cakes, and a jar of honey and go
to him . . .*   1 Kings 14:3

1 teaspoon fennel seeds	$\frac{1}{2}$ teaspoon baking soda
2 eggs	Pinch of salt
$\frac{1}{4}$ pound butter	$\frac{3}{4}$ cup honey
$2\frac{1}{2}$ cups whole wheat flour	1 egg, beaten

Toast the fennel seeds for 5 minutes in an oven heated to
400°F. Set aside. In a mixing bowl, combine eggs, butter, flour,
soda, salt, and the honey until well blended. Spread in an
oiled 12-×-8-inch pan (Pyrex is best for this). Bake for 20
minutes in an oven preheated to 350°F. Remove cake from
oven. Immediately brush top with beaten egg and sprinkle
on toasted fennel seeds.

Saffron Cake

. . . spikenard and saffron . . . with all the chief spices
Song of Solomon 4:14

$\frac{1}{8}$ teaspoon saffron	$\frac{1}{2}$ teaspoon baking soda
1 cup milk	1 cup honey
6 eggs, separated	Pinch of salt
$1\frac{3}{4}$ cup whole wheat pastry flour	Zest of one orange, finely chopped
$1\frac{3}{4}$ cup blanched almonds, finely ground	

Soak saffron in milk for one hour.

In a large bowl, beat egg yolks until they form a ribbon. Combine flour, almonds, and salt in one bowl and saffron milk with soda in another. Alternately beat in small amounts of flour mixture and milk mixture. Add honey and orange zest. In a separate bowl, whip egg whites with a pinch of salt until stiff peaks form. Mix ¼ cup of egg whites into batter to loosen. Fold in remainder of egg whites until just mixed. Do not overbeat. Pour into three lightly oiled 8½-×-4½-inch loaf pans. Bake at 350°F for 45 minutes. Remove from oven and let cool for 30 minutes. Run a knife around edge to loosen, then flip onto a rack to cool completely.

Passover Spice Cake

For seven days no leaven shall be found in your houses for whoever eats what is leavened, that same person shall be cut off from the congregation of Israel . . .   Exodus 12:19

The ancient Passover prohibition against leavening led to the development of holiday cakes made with matzah meal and eggs.

1 cup honey	⅓ cup wine
12 eggs, separated	1½ teaspoons cinnamon
1 cup almonds or walnuts, chopped	1½ cup matzah cake meal or finely crumbed crackers

Preheat oven to 325°F. In a small saucepan gently warm honey. In a mixing bowl, beat egg yolks, almonds, wine, cinnamon, matzah cake meal, and warmed honey. In a separate bowl, beat egg whites to stiff peaks. Fold whites into batter slowly. Pour batter into ungreased standard 9- or 10-inch tube pan or two loaf pans. Bake for an hour. Test for doneness: an inserted knife or clean broom straw should come out dry. Up to 10 additional minutes of baking time may be necessary.

Carob-Honey Sponge Cake

Carob flour, the powdered pod of the carob tree, is also called St. John's bread because of the legend that in the wilderness John the Baptist ate only carob pods and honey.

1 cup whole wheat pastry
  flour
½ cup carob flour
2 teaspoons cinnamon
6 eggs, separated
⅓ cup softened butter

½ cup honey
⅓ cup water
2 teaspoons wine or grape
  juice

Combine flour, carob, and cinnamon, mixing well. Beat egg yolks, add butter and honey, and mix well. Add water and wine or grape juice to egg mixture. Combine the two mixtures and stir thoroughly. In a separate bowl, beat the egg whites until they form stiff peaks. Fold egg whites gently into batter. Do not overbeat.

Preheat oven to 300°F. Carob must be cooked at low temperature to prevent burning. Pour batter into oiled 9-inch spring-form pan and bake for 1¼ hours or into two loaf pans 7 or 8 inches long and bake for one hour and 5 minutes. Test for doneness: when a clean straw or knife inserted into the center comes out dry, the cake is done. As with all honey cakes, this one keeps well.

Honey Cheesecake

Among the many cultural gifts of the Greeks to the Holy Land may have been cheesecake, the declaimed favorite of her poets and philosophers.

3 tablespoons pine nuts
2 cups ricotta cheese
1 cup honey
4 eggs, lightly beaten
$\frac{3}{4}$ teaspoon cinnamon
$\frac{1}{2}$ teaspoon lemon rind, grated

3 tablespoons almonds, slivered
1 whole wheat pie crust (optional, see below)

Preheat oven to 350°F. Toast pine nuts on a baking sheet for 5 minutes. Mix cheese, honey, eggs, cinnamon, and lemon rind with wire whisk. Chop the pine nuts and almonds and add to mixture. Batter may be prepared by combining all ingredients in a food processor. Pour into the whole wheat pie crust or into an oiled pie plate or spring-form pan. Bake for an hour and 10 minutes. Refrigerate.

Whole Wheat Pie Crust

. . . fine flour as a daily grain offering . . . It shall be made in a pan with oil. When it is well-mixed, you shall bring it in . . .
Leviticus 6:20–21

7 tablespoons butter
2 cups whole wheat pastry flour

1 teaspoon salt
4 tablespoons cold water

Work butter into flour and salt with hands, until mixture forms small pea-sized balls. Add water and blend lightly. Form into a ball. Dough may be rolled out at this point, but it is easier to handle if refrigerated for 30 minutes.

On a floured board, roll out dough to a circle slightly larger than the pie pan. Gently lift and place dough into the oiled pie pan. Breaks in the dough can be pinched or patched together.

For honey cheesecake: Prick dough with fork in several places, sprinkle top of pie crust with dry beans or small clean pebbles, and bake for 8 minutes in an oven preheated to 400°F. Remove beans or pebbles and bake another 2 to 3 minutes. To cook completely, leave pie crust in oven for 20 to 30 minutes, taking care not to burn.

Sweet Millet Balls

Finger foods such as these dainty sweetmeats were the preferred way to serve desserts or snacks in the ancient Middle East, where there were few forks or spoons. The Children of Israel washed their hands before praying and always prayed before eating.

1½ cups chopped dried fruit (raisins, figs, apricots, dates—⅓ cup of each is a good combination)
1 cup cooked millet (see page 103)

½ cup chopped walnuts
½ cup chopped or ground almonds

If dried fruit is unusually dry, cover and soak in boiling water for an hour. Combine chopped fruit (vary proportions to taste if desired), cooked millet, and walnuts. Shape the sticky mixture into balls about one inch in diameter. Roll balls between hands until smooth. Dip the balls in chopped or ground almonds. Makes about 32 little balls. Refrigerate. This recipe is easy and fun for children.

Ashurey

Noah and his family knew that the flood was ending when a dove returned to the ark with an olive branch (Genesis 8:11). According to legend, all the remaining food was made into a sweet pudding called ashurey.

1 cup cooked chickpeas
   (canned may be used)
½ cup bulghar wheat
¼ cup millet
¼ cup barley
6 cups water
¾ cup milk
¾ cup honey
1 tablespoon salt
¼ cup raisins
¼ cup figs, cut up and
   stemmed

¼ cup dates, pitted and cut
   up
¼ cup dried apricot pieces
¼ cup almonds, in small
   pieces
¼ cup walnut pieces
Dash of rose water (or to
   taste)
Yogurt or whipped cream

Cook chickpeas, bulghar, millet, and barley in the water for one hour or until barley is tender. Add the milk, honey, salt, raisins, figs, dates, and apricots. Stir and simmer for ½ hour. Add the almonds, walnuts, and rose water. Turn off the heat and stir. Serve hot or cold, garnished with yogurt or whipped cream. Vary proportions to taste.

Raisin, Barley and Apricot Pudding

. . . they shall bake the grain offering . . .   Ezekiel 46:20

1 cup barley
2 cups water
½ cup dried apricots
½ cup white raisins
½ cup dark raisins

¼ cup honey
½ teaspoon powdered ginger
¼ teaspoon cinnamon
Yogurt

Cook the barley in 1 cup water for 30 minutes. Drain. In a large bowl, cover the apricots and raisins with 1 cup water and let sit for 10 minutes. Add the partially cooked barley, honey, and spices. Blend well. Pour the mixture into an oiled baking pan, dot with butter, and bake at 350°F for 40 minutes. Serve warm or cold, topped with yogurt.

Honey-Fried Nuts

I went down to the garden of nuts . . .   Song of Solomon 6:11

¾ cup honey
1 teaspoon Fish Sauce (See page 73)
1 tablespoon vinegar or lemon juice

1 cup whole almonds or walnut halves
Butter or oil for frying

Combine honey, Fish Sauce, and vinegar or juice. Marinate the nuts in this mixture at least 2 hours, or overnight. Drain. In a small pan, heat enough oil or butter to just cover the nuts. Fry a few at a time. Cook until just golden. Remove and drain. Serve at the end of a meal, after other desserts.

Pistachio Almond Cookies

. . . a little honey, spices, and myrrh, pistachio nuts and almonds. Genesis 43:11

2 cups almonds, shelled
1 cup pistachio nuts, shelled
½ cup grape or apple juice

½ teaspoon cinnamon
1 cup honey
1 teaspoon salt

Grind nuts to meal in a blender or food processor, a few at a time if necessary. Add juice to make a smooth paste. Add cinnamon, honey, and salt. Drop onto an oiled baking sheet and press into rounds. Bake in a preheated oven at 300°F for 10 minutes or until golden. These cookies burn easily, so watch carefully.

Almond Honey Paste

. . . Behold the rod of Aaron had sprouted and put forth buds, had produced blossoms and yielded ripe almonds. Numbers 17:8

2 cups boiling water
1 pound almonds
5 to 8 tablespoons Amaretto
 or other almond liqueur
1 cup honey

1 cup water
Few drops of rose water
 (optional)
2 egg whites, stiffly beaten

Pour the boiling water over the almonds and drain. Remove skins if desired. Grind nuts in a food processor or meat grinder to a smooth oily paste. (They may need to be ground a few times to achieve this consistency.) Add the Amaretto or other liqueur.

Heat the honey and water until a drop of the hot syrup in a cup of cool water will form a soft ball (240°F on a candy thermometer). Add the ground almonds, rose water, and almond liqueur. Remove from heat and add the egg whites. Pack into jars and refrigerate. Use as a spread on bread or cookies.

Almond Pistachio Paste

In the recipe above, subtract ½ cup almonds and add ½ cup pistachios. Add more honey to taste.

Pistachio Snow Sherbet

At the royal Persian banquets, one refreshed the palate between courses with snow sherbets.

1 quart clean, uncompacted
   snow
2 cups fresh grape juice
1 cup pistachio nuts,
   blanched and shelled

Few drops of rose water
2 tablespoons honey
   (optional)

Store snow in freezer until ready to use. In a small saucepan, boil grape juice until liquid is reduced by about half. In a mortar or blender, grind pistachio nuts to a paste. Add rose water and sweeten with the honey if desired. Add nut mixture to grape syrup. When mixture has cooled, spoon over mounds of fresh, clean snow.

Honeyed Cream

Honey and milk are under your tongue . . .   Song of Solomon 4:11

1 pint heavy cream, clotted cream, sour cream, or unflavored yogurt

$\frac{1}{4}$ cup honey (or more if desired)

In small bowls place individual portions of cream or yogurt. Pass around a bowl of honey so each person can stir in a few tablespoons. Serve the cream gently warmed on a cold night, whipped and cooled on a warm night. Biblical households had small wooden bowls used exclusively to serve milk and honey at the end of meals.

Goat Cheese Pancakes With Fennel Seed

Fennel seed is a licoricelike spice indigenous to the Bible lands. Anise seed may be substituted.

$\frac{1}{4}$ cup goat cheese
$\frac{1}{4}$ cup cottage cheese
$\frac{1}{4}$ teaspoon fennel seed
  (more if desired)
3 eggs, separated

$\frac{1}{2}$ cup whole wheat pastry
  flour
Salt and pepper to taste
Butter or oil

In a small bowl mash cheeses and fennel seed with a fork. Add egg yolks, flour, salt and pepper, and blend. In a separate bowl, beat egg whites until stiff and fold into the cheese and yolks. Heat and oil a griddle. Pour small circles of batter, as with regular pancakes. Brown and turn to brown on second side. Serve with Almond Paste or Grape Honey.

Biblical Cheeses and Fruits

As with many foods that flourish in the same location, goat and sheep cheeses are wonderful with biblical fruits.

Try dates, apricots, or figs arranged on a tray with a variety of mild, fresh goat cheeses.

A cluster of small grape-sized white cheese balls can be served with clusters of red, green, and black grapes.

Watermelon and sheep cheese is an unexpectedly good combination.

Muskmelons go well with any spiced or marinated cheese, as does citrus fruit.

Decorate a mound of white cheese with fresh pomegranate seeds.

Dress fresh fruit Roman-style with black pepper. Black pepper sometimes cost the equivalent of $125 a pound in imperial Rome and was savored against the mild, sweet background of the finest fresh fruits.

Stuff curd cheeses into dates, figs, and stoned prunes. Top each piece with an almond or pistachio.

Spread fresh or toasted whole wheat bread with a mild white cheese. Top with slices of fresh figs or fresh or dried dates.

A pita pocket stuffed with fresh cheese and seedless grapes or Grape Honey is a wholesome lunch or snack for a youngster.

"Frost" a melon slice with creamy yogurt cheese.

Pack demispoonfuls of white cheese into pitted dates or prunes. Deep-fry for 5 minutes. Sprinkle with toasted almonds and serve with hot milk flavored with honey and cinnamon.

Watermelon In Ginger Wine

Watermelon was indigenous to the Nile Valley, whereas ginger was an exotic imported spice. The classical writer Theophrastus mentions the use of ginger to flavor wine.

$\frac{1}{2}$ watermelon
$\frac{1}{2}$ cup dry white wine
1 cup water

1 tablespoon honey
2 small pieces candied ginger, grated

Use melon baller or cut seeded watermelon into bite-size chunks. Combine wine, water, and honey. Heat gently. Add ginger. Let cool. Pour mixture over watermelon. Refrigerate for several hours. Green ginger wine may be substituted for wine, honey, and candied ginger.

Fresh Berry Purée

. . . and come upon them in front of the mulberry trees.
                                                    2 Samuel 5:23

2 pounds fresh mulberries, washed (fresh strawberries, raspberries, blackberries, or boysenberries can be substituted)
$\frac{1}{4}$ cup honey (or to taste)

$\frac{1}{8}$ teaspoon salt
2 tablespoons vinegar or lemon juice
1 cup heavy cream or yogurt (optional)

Put half of the berries in a heavy saucepan with the honey, salt, and juice. Cook gently to a rich, syrupy mash, adding more honey if necessary. Fifteen minutes is about enough time for mulberries. Watch the fruit carefully for doneness. Remove from heat, cool for fifteen minutes, and stir in the remaining fresh berries. Refrigerate if not serving immediately. Whip cream if desired and fold in cream or yogurt before serving.

Figs in Red Wine and Cream

. . . as also wine, grapes and figs . . . Nehemiah 13:15

2 cups sweet red wine
3 tablespoons honey
1 pound dried figs

1 cup heavy cream
Ground cinnamon

In a saucepan, bring red wine and honey to a boil. Add figs and turn down to a simmer. Simmer figs for an hour. Turn off heat and let cool. Add cream, whipped if desired, and serve in bowls with a dash of cinnamon.

Haroseth

This Passover fruit dish symbolizes the mortar the Hebrew slaves used in building the Egyptian pyramids.

3 cups apples, chopped
$\frac{3}{4}$ cup almonds or walnuts, chopped
$\frac{3}{4}$ cup sweet red wine or grape juice

$\frac{1}{2}$ teaspoon cinnamon
$\frac{1}{2}$ cup dates, chopped
$\frac{1}{2}$ cup raisins

Combine all ingredients. Serve immediately or chill for several hours. There are many variations of this recipe.

The Fruit Sweeteners of Antiquity: Grape Honey and Must

The grape honeys used in the ancient world were the equivalent of our unsugared jams and jellies. The natural fruit sugars are concentrated by boiling the grapes down to a pulpy syrup. Sweet grapes naturally produce a sweeter syrup with less cooking, while tart, underripe grapes produce tart grape honeys which are excellent condiments for meat and poultry.

Wash grapes and place in a saucepan with a small amount of water ($\frac{1}{2}$ cup water to 4 cups grapes). Boil about 20 minutes or until thick. Strain if grape seeds are present. Store in sterilized jars or in refrigerator.

Must is made by adding crushed mustard seed to grape honey. The exact proportions vary according to taste. To every cup of grape honey add 1 teaspoon dried mustard. See page 11 for an additional must recipe.

Apricot Curd

½ pound dried apricots,   Water to cover
  chopped *or*
6 ounces apricot leather

In a saucepan, cover dried apricots with water and simmer, stirring frequently, until a thick syrup is formed. Refrigerate.

Date Syrup

¼ pound dates, pitted   ½ cup water

In a saucepan, combine dates and water and simmer on low heat until dates are soft. Mash dates into water and cook until a thick syrup is formed. Refrigerate.

SUGGESTED MENUS

Egyptian Banquet Menu

T he Egyptian empire was over two thousand years old when Abraham and Sarah first lived at the Pharaoh's court (Genesis 12). The Egyptians ate well, as the marshes of the Nile yielded abundant fish, waterfowl, and aquatic vegetables (such as the lotus). The well-irrigated Nile Valley exported grain throughout the ancient world, requiring supervision by provident administrators like Joseph (Genesis 41). According to biblical chronology the Hebrews lived in Egypt for four hundred years.

Egyptian-Style Fava Bean Soup
Cornish Game Hens With Nuts
Duck in Grape Juice
Fried Fish in Radish Sauce
Whole Baked Garlic
Poached Lotus Roots
Cucumbers Stuffed With Barley and Raisins
Beer Bread

Fig Pastries
Watermelon With Ginger

King Solomon's Feast

And when the Queen of Sheba had seen all the wisdom of Solomon, and the house that he had built, the food on his table, the seating of his servants, the service of his waiters and their apparel, his cupbearers, and his entry way by which he went up to the houses of the Lord, there was no more spirit in her.

Kings 10:4–5

All the foods in this menu are found in the Song of Solomon.

Grilled Marinated Quail
Saddle of Venison With Hot Apricot Sauce
Rack of Lamb With Must Sauce
Saffron Pilav
Red Cabbage With Raisins
Apricot Raisin Sourdough Bread
Green Salad
Fresh Fig and Grape Salad
Saffron Cake
Hot Wine Spiced With Cinnamon

Babylonian Banquet

Belshazzar the king made a great feast for a thousand of his lords and drank wine in the presence of the thousand.   Daniel 5:1

The fertile valleys of the Tigris and Euphrates Rivers contained a number of city states, collectively known as Mesopotamia, which was home to the world's first civilization. The descendants of Noah lived in Shinar (Genesis 11:2) and Abraham began his wanderings with Sarah from Ur, capital of the Chaldeans (Genesis 11:31). Periodically, one group within Mesopotamia such as the Babylonians rose up and conquered its neighbors. 1 Chronicles, 2 Chronicles, and 2 Kings record the Babylonian conquest of the Holy Land, beginning in 840 B.C.

Among the Mesopotamian writings are lists of produce from the royal garden of King Merodach-Baladan, who is twice mentioned in the Bible (Isaiah 39:1 and 2 Kings 20:12). The Mesopotamians had much the same diet as the Hebrews, with a few variations. And they were very fond of beer, a drink not mentioned in the Bible. Sesame was widely cultivated, the oil being preferred for cooking, and sesame seeds were a popular flavoring and garnish. Pistachio nuts were plentiful and pale green pistachio wood paneled the royal palaces. The date palm was extensively cultivated, providing fruit, wine, wood, and the delectable hearts of palm among its myriad uses.

Roast Chicken Stuffed With Fried Onions and Nuts
Lamb Stew With Quinces and Pears
Perch With Tahini Sauce
Sumerian Watercress
Tabbouleh Salad
Hearts of Palm With Yogurt Sesame Sauce
Date Nut Bread
Pistachio Almond Paste
Dates stuffed with white cheese, fried in sesame oil
Assorted dark and light beers

Persian Banquet

The Persians overthrew the Babylonian empire in 539 B.C. and allowed the captive Israelites to return home and reestablish Jerusalem. The Books of Ezra and Nehemiah chronicle the Persian period from 546 B.C. to 334 B.C. The Book of Esther tells of life in the elegant Persian court and the many feasts, including one lasting one hundred and eighty days (Esther 1:4).

Persia was a land of luscious fruits, including the cherry, peach, plum, and apple. The walnut was called the Persian nut in honor of its presumed place of origin. Situated between the Middle and Far East, the Persians imported rice, spinach, exotic spices, and chicken from China and India to the Mediterranean area.

Persian cooking was renowned throughout the ancient world for its delicate spicing and rich sauces combining fruit and nuts. A banquet would include many wines and mountain snow sherbets topped with fruit syrups.

Caviar from the Caspian Sea
Persian Yogurt Soup With Meatballs
Poached Fish With Capers
Duck With Pomegranate Walnut Sauce
Roast Beef With Horseradish Walnut Sauce
Saffron Pilav
Steamed Spinach
Snow Sherbet served between courses
Baked Apples With Cinnamon
Raisin Cake
Wines

Deipnosophists—Greek Banquet of the Learned

In 334 B.C., the Greeks, led by Alexander the Great, defeated the Persians and took control of their empire, including the Holy Land. The intellectual Greek culture, with its art, literature, and philosophy, profoundly influenced the Israelites. Conversely, the Greeks were very receptive to the Hebrew Scriptures and translated them. Many Greeks converted to Christianity during the time of Paul.

In dietary matters, the Greeks were concerned with health, exercise, and balance. How much one ate, in what combination of foods, and at what time of day were as important to the Greeks as the specific menu. The Greeks were fond of shrimp, rabbit, herbed broths, flax breads, black puddings, and cheesecake. Intelligent dinner conversation and good wine were as important to the educated Greeks as the food.

Sardines Grilled in Vine Leaves
Cream of Barley Soup
Savory Stew With Lentils and Raisins
Cornish Hens in Greek Citrus Marinade
Baked Celery and Fennel
Mint Salad
Honey Cheesecake
Fresh melon
A selection of wines

An Essene Vegetarian Meal

The Dead Sea Scrolls are manuscripts from the Essene religious sect. They testify to the many similarities between the early Christians and the Essenes. Jesus grew up near an Essene community, and some of the Apostles may have been Essenes. The Essenes lived in self-sufficient collectives and were primarily vegetarians. Members dressed in white for the communal meals, which usually included sprouted bread and wine.

Vegetable Soup With Whole Grains
Three Bean Soup
An assortment of Sprouted Essene Breads made with figs,
    raisins, seeds, and nuts
Leeks and Cabbage
Hot Goat Cheese With Fresh Herb Salad
Sweet Millet Balls
Wine
Pomegranates and fresh figs

Wedding Feast

On the third day there was a wedding in Cana of Galilee, and the mother of Jesus was there. Now both Jesus and His disciples were invited to the wedding.   John 2:1–2

Assorted spiced cheeses with matzah:
    Cinnamon Cheese
    Black Cumin Cheese Spread
    Hot Radish Cheese Spread
Sabbath Fish Balls

Crown Roast of Lamb With Pomegranate Raisin Sauce
Duckling With Must Sauce
Millet Pilav
Arugola Rose Salad
Orange, Onion, and Olive Salad
Tray of dried apricots, dates, and almonds
Shaped breads: braids, triangles, rolls
Honey Wine Cake
Fresh fruit
Wine

Roman Banquet

The rise of the Roman Empire and the birth of Christianity
are interwoven. Because he was a Roman citizen, Paul, the
great missionary, was privileged to travel throughout the
Empire to the early churches.

The extravagance of the Roman banquet table is legendary. Influence and power were negotiated through extraordinary feasts. An impressive appetizer of peacock tongues
might require the demise of two hundred birds. In fact, laws
were passed limiting the extravagance of banquets, but as
might be expected, enforcement of this culinary moderation
proved difficult.

Romans loved spicy foods, and their casseroles typically
combined several meats, fish, poultry, cheese, vegetables,
and herbs in one dish. Garum, the fermented anchovy
sauce, appeared in almost every savory recipe. While the Romans introduced many dining customs and foods into their
colonies, they preferred imported specialties from all cor-
ners of the known world.

Hard-Boiled Eggs With Horseradish Walnut Cream
Broccoli Goat Cheese Soup
Roast Ham With Sweet Sauces
Roman Beef Sauté With Onions
Grilled Fish With Garlic and Anchovy
Leeks and Cabbage
Roman Asparagus
Rose Apple Salad
Whole Wheat Sourdough Bread
Marinated Goat Cheeses
Hot wine scented with honey and cinnamon
Plums, apples, and roasted chestnuts
Honey-fried Nuts

Agape Fish Dinner

The early Christians often met for fellowship meals known as Agape. In contrast to the extravaganzas of the pagan Romans, the Christians tried to maintain a modest and dignified tone as Paul exhorts in the Epistle of Jude. Fish, because it was a symbol of the early church, is thought to have been standard fare at the Agape table along with vegetables and fresh breads.

Anchovy Toast
Barley Stew With Lentils
Broiled Fish With Honey and Onions
Grilled Saint Peter's Fish
Coriander Relish
Barley Wheat Sourdough Bread
Raisin Cake
Fresh grapes

Passover Dinner

Passover is one of the Jewish festivals, richest in tradition. Passover recalls the exodus of the Hebrews from Egyptian bondage under the grace of God and has become a symbol of liberation from slavery for many peoples. Jesus instructed the preparation of the Passover feast (Luke 22:8), which became known as the Last Supper. Passover incorporated an older celebration, The Feast of Unleavened Bread, retaining and elaborating the custom of eating no leavened products during the Passover week. The order of courses is based on the Roman banquet, including wine, raw vegetables and a first course of eggs. Before and after the Passover dinner, the Passover service, or seder, is performed. The Haggadah is the book read during this time-honored religious service.

Hard-boiled eggs with saltwater dip
Raw vegetable platter: parsley, celery stalks, olives, grated
    horseradish mixed with vinegar as a dip
Matzah
Sabbath Fish Balls
Whole Roast Suckling Lamb or Leg of Lamb
    With Cumin and Mustard
Green Salad of "Bitter Herbs"
Endive With Olives and Raisins
Haroseth
Passover Spice Cake
Wine or grape juice

Easter Dinner

Easter is not specifically mentioned in the Scriptures, but the celebration of the resurrection of Jesus evolved from Passover and became one of the first holy days of the early Christians. As with Passover, Easter incorporates some of the Roman dining customs. Ham, a favorite of Roman feasts, was served along with the traditional Paschal Lamb. Eggs, an ancient symbol of the rebirth of spring, became part of the Easter celebration.

Salty Sweet Eggs
Anchovy Toast
Ham Steaks With Figs
Roast Suckling Lamb, Fatted Calf, or Stuffed Breast
      of Lamb With Raisin Sauce
Parched Wheat (Bulghar) Pilav
Green Salad
Apricot Raisin Bread
Fresh Yogurt Cheese
Candied Beets
Honey Cake

Pentecost Dinner

Pentecost is an ancient agricultural festival that for centuries coincided with the first wheat harvest of the Holy Land, seven weeks after the first barley harvest. The entire fifty days between Passover and Pentecost were celebrated by the early Christian church with feasting, as opposed to the fasting that preceded Easter. Pentecost, considered to mark the beginning of the Christian church, was the time described in Acts 2 when the Holy Spirit came to the Apostles, as some one hundred and twenty disciples gathered for the festival in Jerusalem.

Pentecost, called Shabuot in the Jewish religion, celebrates the giving of the Ten Commandments on Mount Sinai. Dairy foods are traditionally eaten out of respect for the Commandment "Thou Shalt Not Kill."

Yogurt With Fresh Herbs and Cucumbers
Barley Stew With Lentils
Saffron Pilav
Hot Goat Cheese With Fresh Herb Salad
Roman Asparagus
Whole Wheat Pitas
Figs in Red Wine With Cream
Fennel Seed Cake
Honey Cheese Cake
Toasted Almonds
Fresh Berry Purée
Wine and grape juice

Chanukah

Chanukah, the Feast of Lights, occurs around the time of the winter solstice and celebrates the miracle of lights during the liberation of the Judaea from the Greek ruler Antiochus Epiphanes. The story is told in 1 and 2 Maccabees of the Apocrypha. The early Christian church held a festival of the Maccabees in August to commemorate this heroic struggle against paganism. Foods cooked in oil recall the oil used to light the eternal light in the restored Temple.

Assorted relishes: olives, pickles, and radishes
Roast Goose Stuffed With Raisins and Barley
Red Cabbage With Raisins
Goat Cheese Pancakes With Fennel Seed
Almond Paste
Sweet-and-Sour Beets on a Bed of Beet Greens
Onion Boards
Figs in Red Wine
Honey Cake

Sabbath Meal

The Sabbath celebrates God's creation of the world. In Exodus 31:17, God specifies that keeping the Sabbath ". . . is a sign between Me and the Children of Israel forever . . ." Ancient wisdom rationalized that the imitation of God in his moral attributes was the measure of a righteous person. Therefore, if God rested on the seventh day from His labors of worldly creation, should not mortals do the same? Whether Saturday, or Sunday, the concept of setting aside one day for religious observance is unquestioned. The Greeks and Romans ridiculed the Hebrews and early Christians for wasting one seventh of their lives in idleness, as this concept went against the prevailing pagan work ethic.

Traditionally, the Sabbath meals were prepared before sundown. Strict observance forbade any man, woman, child, or servant to work in the home or out. Even the farm animals rested on the Sabbath. Jesus attended synagogue and read for the Sabbath in Luke 4:16.

1 Sabbath Dinner
Sabbath Fish Balls
Chicken With Sage in a Clay Pot
Sweet-and-Sour Beets on a Bed of Beet Greens
Basic Barley
Figs in Red Wine
Challah
Fennel Seed Cake

2 Sabbath Lunch and Supper
Classic Sabbath Casserole
Challah
Fresh fruit

Children's Bible Meals and Snacks

1

Matzah
Cinnamon Cheese
Chopped dates and almonds
Grape juice

2

Yogurt Soup With Raisins
Tabbouleh Fish Cakes
Apricot nectar diluted with water

3

Barley and Whole Wheat Sourdough Bread
Lamb Shish Kebabs
Baked Onions
Dried Apricots

4

Sabbath Fish Balls
Lentil Pancakes With Grape Honey
Cold creamed beet and carob yogurt drinks
Watermelon

THE
SCRIPTURAL GARDENER:
GROWING AND DRYING
BIBLICAL PRODUCE

✠   ✠   ✠   ✠

ome of the common food plants of the Bible, which
are not always available in American markets, are easy to grow.
People in biblical times were obliged to select nature's hardiest plants, and particularly those that yielded storageable
foods. The simple agricultural processes that every man,
woman, and child understood formed the basis of many biblical metaphors and images. You can grow and store these
foods in the same natural ways, recalling the lifestyles of the
people of the Bible. The following notes are meant as sug-
gestions to give the home gardener a sense of the possibili-
ties. Many plants of the Bible such as cos (romaine) lettuce,
cucumbers, peas, celery, zucchini, and herbs such as sage and
oregano are well known to home gardeners.

Vegetables

ARUGOLA

Arugola, also known as Rockette or Rocket lettuce, is a pungent salad green that grows easily and reseeds itself if allowed. It prefers cooler climates. Cut off the leaves, but not the roots, and the plant will regenerate. Arugola is generally eaten raw, but can be lightly steamed.

CARDOON

The cardoon is a beautiful thistle with irregular green edging on thick white edible stalks that taste like artichoke hearts, a close relative of the cardoon. In zones 7, 8, and 9 the cardoon is perennial, as in the Holy Land. It can be grown anywhere in the United States if treated as an annual and planted in well-drained enriched soil. Start indoors in the north at the same time as tomatoes. Keep moist. When planting, allow three feet between plants or seeds as they become quite large. Cardoons require 120 to 150 days to mature. Since aphids may be a problem, hose off regularly and use an organic product to discourage them, such as rotenone. When growing as a perennial, leave the base in the ground after cutting the leaves so that the plant will winter over. The next summer the cardoon will become an ornamental with thistles and then extraordinary blue flowers on a tall stalk. New vegetable growth will appear at the base.

CORIANDER

Coriander yields delicious pungent seeds for spicing, green leaves (sometimes called cilantro or Chinese parsley) used as an herb, and edible roots. It needs only two months to produce edible leaves and can be raised indoors in pots if there is sufficient sun. Allow coriander to go to seed if the seeds are to be used for seasoning. Try the fresh green leaves, an important ingredient in many of our recipes. Coriander does not dry well.

FAVA BEANS

Fava beans, a winter crop in ancient Palestine, have a unique taste resembling chestnuts. They require three frost-free months and can be grown in many temperate zones. (Their long growing season makes them unsuitable for cold climates and extreme heat injures their delicate flowers).

Plant about one inch deep, 4 to 6 inches apart, in blocks of at least 4 rows with about a foot between each row so that the vines will be able to intertwine and support each other. A fence or trellis can be used. The attractive white flowers are tipped with black but require frequent pinching off to promote pod production and discourage aphids.

When the beans are the size of green peas and the pods finger-thin, they may be cooked whole. When medium-size, the beans are shelled, a process made easier by parboiling in the shell for 10 minutes, then discarding the fuzz-lined pods. When large, favas are still edible but require a double shelling which is why large dry beans are often sold with the inner bean skin removed. Parboil fresh, large beans for 10 to 20 minutes, pour off the hot water, and cool in fresh water. Then press off the skins by pushing one side of each cooked bean so that it slips out of its skin. Or peel raw. The process is much easier and faster than it sounds, especially with a little practice.

LEEKS

Leeks are a mild, sweet onion, highly prized in Mediterranean cooking. Leeks can be expensive to buy, but are very easy to grow in many climates. A light soil is best. They are planted outdoors early or started in flats. Since the tiny green shoots are easily mistaken for grass or weeds, they must be carefully marked. They are best planted in a trench so that the soil level can be built up gradually. This encourages development of the white part of the stalk, which is the most flavorful. The leeks grow slowly and by autumn will be usable although quite thin. In the northeast United States, leeks winter well and can be pulled whenever needed. Pull the largest ones first and take them alternately so that that remaining plants will have more space to grow.

MINT

Mints are easily grown perennials. They can be planted in pots and wintered near a sunny window. Mint is difficult to sprout and hence most easily grown from cuttings.

MUSTARD

Mustard grows easily and quickly in a variety of climates. The leaves, flowers, and seeds are edible. If grown for seed, pick the pods before they are quite ripe or the seed may scatter as the dry pods open. Try the young leaves in salad; stew the older leaves for up to 45 minutes. Season with vinegar.

LOTUS

Lotus (Nelumbium) is planted late in the Spring in ponds or streams for its edible roots. If the magnificent lotus flowers are the main object, it can be grown in 18-inch tubs. Start with young tubers, available from nurseries which specialize in aquatic plants. Handle them with care so as not injure their delicate brittle tips. Plant two inches below the soil bottom, in well-manured soil, barely covering the growing tips with a water depth of about six inches. The creeping rootstock will grow to ten to fifteen feet with new tubers at intervals. In Egypt, lotus was undoubtedly grown at the edge of the Nile, where the white tubers could be harvested easily. Artificial ponds can be used, if they are large enough to accommodate the roots. In a small space, the roots will not develop sufficiently to produce a good crop of tubers. As long as the roots are below the frost line, they are perfectly hardy.

PARSLEY

Flat-leaved parsley is the authentic Middle Eastern variety known as Italian parsley. It is darker and stronger in flavor than the curly variety, although grown the same way. Anise is a member of the parsley family and grown in the same way.

SORREL

Sorrel, one of the bitter herbs, grows wild in sandy, somewhat acid soils. A cultivated version with larger leaves can be planted as a garden crop. Sorrel is also called sour grass and sour dock. Because of its high oxalic acid content, it is more nutritious when cooked. Break off the flower stems before the flower develops as otherwise the leaves will be tough and extremely acidic.

Fruits

FIGS

Fig trees provided fruit, shade, and beauty. The Trojano, also called the Black Kadota, is one of the common figs of the Bible. The tree gives two crops a year in warm climates, but only one in the north. The prolific Trojano will sometimes bear fruit after one year, while other varieties may require three years before bearing. The fig does not grow well out of doors, north of Washington D.C. Trees up to ten feet can be grown in large containers and brought in for the winter to rest in a garage or cellar. The fig needs a sunny site in any climate. The edible part of the fig is actually the flower which will later bear seed. The famous Smyrna fig needs special pollinating wasps which were imported from Asia Minor to California to facilitate the fig production.

GRAPES

Grape vines offer the same benefits enjoyed in biblical times: pleasurable shade and delicious fruit which can be eaten raw, dried to make raisins, cooked down to make grape honey, or fermented into wine. The biblical grape *vitis vinifera* has a tight skin and a winelike flavor. It requires a very hot summer and winter temperatures above 5°F. Since this grape is close to other modern varieties, grow the one best suited to your climate. Grapes are strong, woody, leafy plants with branches that can extend up to fifty feet. Prune to keep the height about five feet for maximum production. The gardener who wants "to sit under his vine and fig tree" can make an arbor with wooden supports, either free standing or attached to a structure, letting the vines grow longer. It is still necessary to prune heavily before new growth starts each spring to prevent the vines from developing mainly branches and leaves, instead of fruit. Pruning to one stem per branch is usually recommended. Grapes need sun, sandy soil with good drainage, and moisture. Started from plants and cuttings, they will begin to bear fruit the third year. A single vine can be grown in a tub if kept pruned back to the single strongest stem and brought in for the winter.

MELONS

Melons of the Bible included muskmelon, the original cantaloupe, and watermelon, a special favorite in Pharaoh's Egypt. Melons are planted outdoors from seed when the soil warms early or started indoors, since muskmelons require 60 to 110 days to mature, depending on climate. They require space for the vines, well-drained soil with constant moisture and sunshine. Often planted in hills or mounds, the plants are thinned to three or four in an area, allowing four feet in each direction for muskmelons and at least six feet for watermelons. In the north, watermelons should be started indoors about a month before the last expected frost and put out about six weeks after starting. Early maturing varieties have been developed.

DRYING FOOD FOR STORAGE

Drying is one of the oldest and most energy-efficient methods of preserving foods. The dry heat of the Holy Land made this method particularly convenient. Herbs can be easily dried on screens in the hot summer sun or in an oven at a very low heat (150°F) with the door partly open, or in a electric food dryer. Another way to recreate the heat of the desert is to put herbs on clean screens or cloths in the back of a station wagon parked in the sun. Herbs can also be tied into bunches and dried by hanging up in a well-ventilated dry room for about a week.

Fruits and vegetables can be dried uncooked. Their bulk will be reduced to about one-sixth to one-third of their original size. Cut into small, uniform pieces and place on screens, trays, or dryers in a single layer. Turn frequently for several days in hot sun. Test for dryness. Herbs when dry will crumble in the hand. Fruits and vegetables can be squeezed with no loss of water. Produce is best left in the air a few extra days before putting away. Apples, apricots, figs, grapes, peaches, pears, prune plums, zucchini, squash, and beans dry well.

Select Bibliography

All biblical references are from *The Holy Bible,* New King James Version, Thomas Nelson (Nashville: 1982).

Ausubel, Nathan, ed. *A Treasury of Jewish Folklore,* Crown Publishers (New York, 1948).

Berman, Louis A. *Vegetarianism and the Jewish Tradition,* KTAV Publishing House Inc. (New York: 1982).

Bothwell, Don and Patricia. *Food in Antiquity,* Praeger (New York: 1969).

Bottero, J., Cassin, E. and Vercoutter, J. *The Near East: Early Civilizations,* Delacourte Press (New York: 1965).

Bouquet, A. C. *Everyday Life in New Testament Times,* Scribner's (New York: 1954).

Bowman, Raymond. *Aramaic Ritual Texts from Persepolis,* University of Chicago: Oriental Institute Publications (Chicago: 1970).

Budge, E. A. Wallis and King, L. W., eds. *Annals of the Kings of Assyria in the British Museum,* The British Museum (London: 1902).

Conteau, Georges. *Everyday Life in Babylonia and Assyria,* Norton (New York: 1966).

Darby, W., Ghaliounqui, P., and Grivetti, L. *Food: The Gift of Osiris,* Academic Press (London: 1979).

Delitzen, Friedrich. *Babel and Bible,* Putnam and Sons (London: 1903).

Dimblesby, Geoffrey. *Plants and Archaeology,* Humanities Press Inc. (New York: 1967).

Dimont, Max. *Jews, God and History,* New American Library (New York: 1962).

Edwards, John. *The Roman Cookery of Apicius,* Hartley and Marks (Washington: 1984).

Forbes, R. J. *Studies in Ancient Technology,* vols. III, IV, V, E. J. Brill (Leiden: 1955).

Ginsburg, Christian D. *The Essenes, Their History and Doctrines,* Routledge and Kegan Paul (London: 1956).

Goor, Asaph. *The History of the Rose in the Holy Land Throughout the Ages,* Massada and Am Hassefer, Ramat-Gan 1970, 1982.

Hedrick, U. P. ed. *Sturtevant's Edible Plants of the World,* Dover Publications (New York: 1972).

Hoffner, Harry A. *Alimenta Hethaeorum: Food Production in Hittite Asia Minor,* American Oriental Society (New Haven: 1974).

Holm, Don and Myrtle. *The Complete Sourdough Cookbook,* Caxton Printers, (Caldwell, Ohio).

Jaffrey, Madhur. *World of the East Vegetarian Cooking,* Alfred Knopf (New York: 1983).

Keating, J. F. *The Agape and the Eucharist,* AMS Press (New York: 1901).

Kenyon, Sir Frederic. *Our Bible and the Ancient Manuscripts,* Harper and Row (New York: 1958).

Kenyon, Kathleen. *Archeology in the Holy Land,* Ernest Benn Ltd (London: 1960).

Kinard, Malvina and Crisler, Janet. *Loaves and Fishes,* Keats Publishing (New Canaan: 1975).

King, Eleanor Anthony. *Bible Plants for American Gardens,* Dover Publications (New York: 1975).

Lehner, Ernst and Johanna. *Folklore and Odysseys of Food and Medicinal Plants,* Tudor Publishing Company, (New York: 1962).

Leonard, Jonathan Norton. *The First Farmers,* Time-Life Books (New York: 1973).

Liebman, Malvina. *Jewish Cookery from Boston to Baghdad,* E. H. Seaman Publishing Company (Miami: 1975).

Maimon, Moses Ben (Maimonides) *The Preservation of Youth,* Philosophical Library (New York: 1958).

Madza, Maidah. *In a Persian Kitchen,* Charles E. Tuttle Company (Rutland, Vermont: 1960).

Mallos, Tess. *The Complete Middle Eastern Cookbook,* McGraw-Hill (New York: 1979).

Mansoor, Menahem. *The Dead Sea Scrolls,* William Eerdmans (New York: 1964).

McKibbin, Jean. *Cookbook of Foods from Biblical Days,* (Salt Lake City: 1971).

McNair, James. *The World of Herbs and Spices,* Robert L. Iacopi (San Francisco: 1979).

Mellart, James. *Earliest Civilizations of the Middle East,* McGraw-Hill (New York: 1965).

Merrill, Selah. *Ancient Jerusalem,* H. Revell Fleming Company (New York: 1908).

Miller, Madeline S. and Lane, Jay. *Harper's Biblical Dictionary,* Harper Brothers (New York: 1952).

Murray, Margaret. *The Splendor That Was Egypt,* Philosophical Library (New York: 1949).

Nathan, Joan. *The Jewish Holiday Kitchen,* Schocken Books (New York: 1979).

Negev, Abraham. *Archaeology in the Land of the Bible,* Schocken Books (New York: 1977).

Plaut, W. G., Bamberger, B. J., and Hallo, W. W. *The Torah: A Modern Commentary,* Union of American Hebrew Congregations (New York: 1981).

Ramazani, Nesta. *Persian Cooking,* Quadrangle Press (New York: 1974).

Roden, Claudia. *A Book of Middle Eastern Food,* Vintage (New York: 1974).

Roebuck, Carl. *The World of Ancient Times,* Scribner's (New York:

1966).

Simon, Marcel. *Jewish Sects in the Time of Jesus,* Fortress Press (Philadelphia: 1967).

Short, A. Rendle. *The Bible and Modern Medicine,* The Paternoster Press (London: 1953).

Storck, John and Teague, Walter Dorwin. *Flour for Man's Bread,* University of Minnesota Press (Minneapolis: 1952).

Strong, James. *The New Strong's Exhaustive Concordance of the Bible,* Thomas Nelson (Nashville: 1984).

Tannahill, Reay. *Food in History,* Stein and Day (New York: 1973).

Thomas, D. Winton. *Documents from Old Testament Times,* Thomas Nelson (New York: 1973).

United Bible Services. *Fauna and Flora of the Bible—Helps for Translators,* London: n.d.

INDEX OF BIBLICAL AND HISTORICAL REFERENCES

INDEX OF FOOD AND RECIPES

Flight Plans

A Bird's-Eye View of Life

Maryjo Koch

Andrews McMeel
Publishing, LLC
Kansas City · Sydney · London

Andrews McMeel Publishing, LLC
an Andrews McMeel Universal company
1130 Walnut Street, Kansas City, Missouri 64106

www.andrewsmcmeel.com

Concept and Design: Jennifer Barry Design, Fairfax, California
Production Assistance: Kristen Wurz

13 14 15 16 17 WKT 10 9 8

ISBN: 978-0-7407-6432-5

Library of Congress Control Number: 2006937594

Attention: Schools and Businesses

Andrews McMeel books are available at quantity discounts with
bulk purchase for educational, business, or sales promotional use.
For information, please e-mail the Andrews McMeel Publishing
Special Sales Department: specialsales@amuniversal.com

Flight Plans

I have always loved birds.

It's easy to see their beauty: Birds' plumage comes in a dizzying array of patterns and colors, from the bright primary hues of Macaws to the dazzling iridescence of Hummingbirds. Their swooping, zipping, and soaring flight is glorious, and their songs are marvels of vocal virtuosity.

In a career of studying and painting birds, nests, and eggs, I have come to see that there is more to birds than mere beauty. Each species is unique and precisely adapted to its environment, whether diving like a Brown Pelican from six stories above the ocean's surface to catch a pouch-full of fish, tap-dancing on improbably blue feet like a Booby to attract a mate, or cradling an egg on Antarctic ice for a months-long incubation like an Emperor Penguin.

Their lives speak to us, perhaps because birds are essential to life on Earth, including our own. They are tightly woven into the fabric of the communities and landscapes we share. Birds seem so at home here: They are who they are, without pretense or artifice. As they skim through the air—literally taking themselves lightly—they exemplify the sayings in this book.

May your life take flight along with theirs!

—Maryjo Koch

Flight Plans

Follow your bliss, but make a flight plan.

The world is your birdbath.

Every calling is great,

when it's greatly sung.

An open mind
collects
the most nectar.

Go out on a limb . . .

it's where the fruit is!

Lead with your strengths!

Wherever you go

make your mark!

Great ideas
need landing gear
as well as wings.

*If at first
you do succeed,
try to hide your
surprise!*

Out of the Nest

There's no place like home to make you
want to fly the coop.

We all have
nuts in
our
family tree!

Most of us have
a rocky start.

Even the biggest bird has
been an egg.

Success

can take a

long time

to hatch.

*It takes
perseverance to
break out of
a shell!*

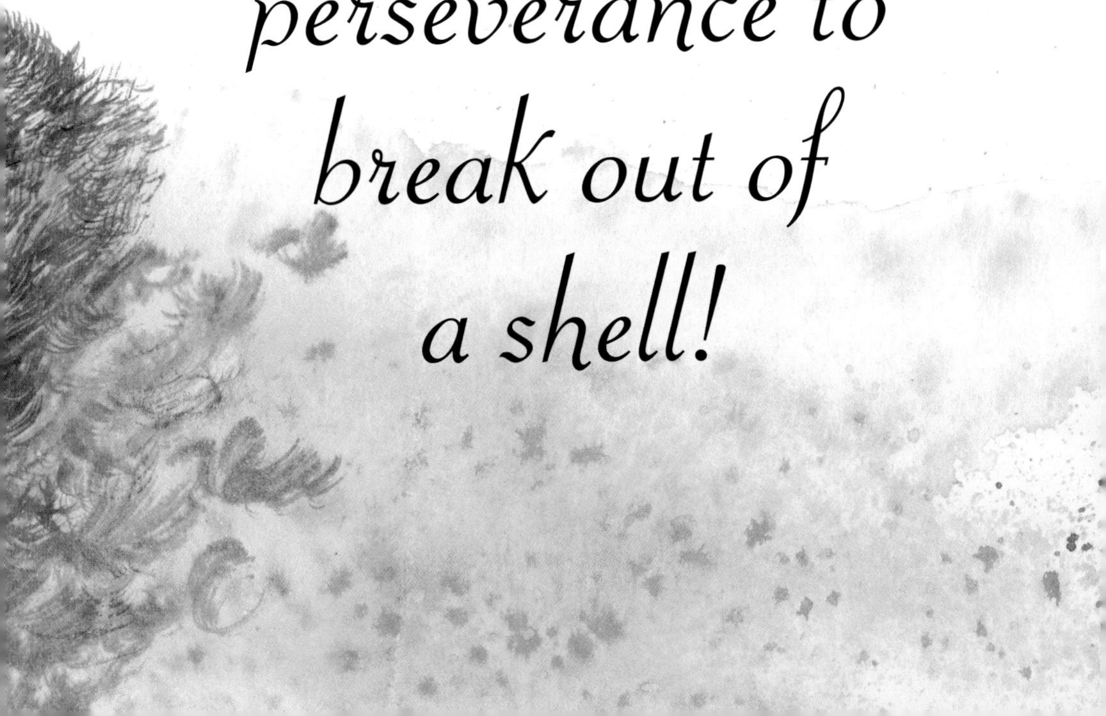

There comes a
time when
we all outgrow
our nests.

New opportunities await you.

If you build it, they will come!

A place is yours when you know where all the twigs go.

Feather your nest
with hard work,
and your nest egg
is sure to grow.

Birds of a Feather

Friendship is the masterpiece of nature.

When you're
out on a limb, it's nice to
be part of a flock.

We all live
under the same sky,
but we don't have
the same horizon.

When birds of a feather
flock together,
the feathers often fly.

It's not only
fine feathers that
make fine
birds.

Relationships require

sticking your neck out.

It takes a long time

to hatch an old friend.

True friends know you're a good egg, even if you're a little cracked!

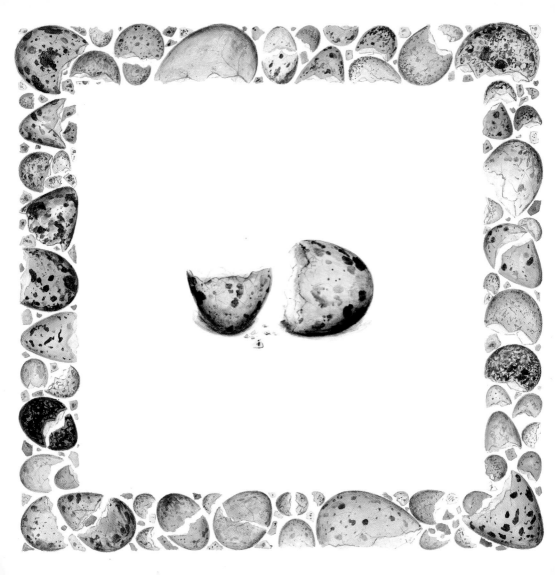

Friendship is a

sheltering tree.

Taking Flight

No bird soars too high if he soars with his own wings.

*You've got to
keep flapping or you'll
fall down!*

Don't be afraid
to make mistakes when
you're trying

your wings.

If you can't do great things, do small things in a great way!

Keep your chin up
when fate clips
your wings.

A smooth sea never

made a skillful sailor.

When things
seem topsy-turvy,
try a new

perspective.

If things get scary,
act like a duck—
be unruffled on the surface,
but paddle like crazy
underneath!

*If you
have too many eggs
in one basket,
find a bigger basket!*

The wiser we get,

how truly bird-the more we can see

brained we can be.

The best vision is
insight,
the best vantage,
a bird's-eye view.

About the Birds

Blue and Gold Macaw
Large, colorful, and noisy, Blue and Gold Macaws are native to rainforests of Central and South America. They are popular in captivity because of their trainability and intelligence. They can be trained to speak with a limited vocabulary of about fifteen words or expressions. Their strong black beaks are used not only for cracking and eating hard nuts and seeds but also as a "third foot" when climbing trees and riverbanks. While they live in monogamous pairs, they travel in large flocks numbering hundreds of birds.

Brown Pelicans
Flying single file with synchronized wingbeats, then elegantly gliding in unison, Pelicans fly unlike any other bird. A Brown Pelican's dive is quite spectacular. From as high as sixty feet, the bird plummets and resurfaces moments later, with catch intact. Internal air chambers cushion the Pelican's impact and help it to surface quickly.

Row of Songbirds
(left to right: Eastern Bluebird, Bohemian Waxwing, American Goldfinch, Northern Cardinal, Indigo Bunting, Summer Tanager, American Robin, Scarlet Tanager, Rufous-sided Towhee) Songbirds are the avian world's virtuosos, genetically fine-tuned instruments for song. Twittering flutes, lilting violins, and flowing clarinets, songbirds perform in open-air arenas, but for the birds, the utterings serve basic functions of life—as territorial markers, danger signals, and mate enticers.

Anna's Hummingbird

Delicate but lightning quick, pennyweight male Hummingbirds are belligerent, territorial, and will tirelessly defend every food source in sight. Hummingbirds can be found almost anywhere flowers bloom . . . especially red ones. It must consume its weight in nectar daily, feeding every ten to fifteen minutes from dawn to dusk. A Hummingbird requires nectar from as many as one thousand fuchsia blossoms to maintain its metabolism for a single day.

American Robin

Although Robins are famous for being expert foragers of earthworms and insects, in winter they eat fruit such as cherries and berries from a variety of berry-producing trees and shrubs. In actuality, a Robin is a Thrush. Early American colonists gave recognition to a bird loosely resembling a breed from the Old World. It came to be known as the American Robin, a distant relative of the European Robin.

Blue-footed Booby

The male Blue-footed Booby entices a mate by putting his best foot forward—literally! He performs an eccentric tap dance with his very bright blue feet combined with elaborate high-stepping to catch his female's eye.

Bird Tracks in Sand

Momentarily earthbound, shorebirds leave their footprints in the sand. A harried Sandpiper shops the waterline; a Pelican lands, then walks awkwardly on webbed feet, as if it finds this human action faintly distasteful. All birds have four toes, except the Ostrich, which has only two.

Mallard Duck Landing

Although Mallards are agile fliers who can take off from the water almost vertically, their large, bright orange webbed feet are equally effective as landing gear. As the ducks come in for a landing their feet provide a platform upon which they can skim the surface of the water, much like water skis. Their feet are also used for propelling the large-bodied birds swiftly through the water. Ducks' legs are set far back on their bodies, providing an advantage in swimming, but making them extremely awkward when walking on land.

Long-eared Owl

Humans may recognize Owls by their charming hoots, ear-splitting screeches, and inquisitive whoo-whoos, but Owls are incomparably silent predators. Softly fringed flight feathers muffle the sound of flapping wings and silence the Owl's deadly approach. It is tough to sneak up on an Owl: Its amazing hearing, augmented by the dish-antenna-shaped "facial disk" of feathers around its eyes and astonishing ability to rotate its head nearly full circle, make it an excellent sentry.

Red-winged Blackbird Nest and Eggs

Red-winged Blackbirds always select either the borders of streams or marshes for their nests. They favor building nests among thick bunches of reeds such as cattails and construct their nests of marsh grass and reeds. They attach their nests to growing marsh vegetation from five to thirteen feet off the ground.

Acorn Woodpecker

Gregarious Acorn Woodpeckers hoard sufficient food to feed their extended family groups by wedging up to fifty thousand nuts into holes made in a centrally located storage tree.

Killdeer Eggs in Rocky Nest

The eggs of a shorebird, which has no nest, are laid directly on the beach. For unwanted predators, it's nearly impossible to find them hiding incognito among the random scheme of shells, pebbles, and debris. Killdeer eggs are mottled with grays and browns to resemble the stones upon which they are laid.

Bird Eggs

The Ostrich lays the largest egg of any bird alive. It is as big as a grapefruit and as heavy as 4,500 Hummingbird eggs, almost 3.3 pounds. The smallest egg of the world's tiniest bird, a Hummingbird, is no larger than a pea and barely nudges the scale at about .02 ounces.

Emperor Penguin with Egg

After laying a single large egg, the Emperor Penguin does not make a nest in the barren Antarctic terrain. Instead the egg is placed right on the male bird's feet, where it is cradled snugly beneath a featherless patch on his belly, which allows his body heat to keep the egg warm. Thousands of duty-bound males huddle together for extra warmth during a grueling two-month incubation while the females feed in the icy Antarctic waters. They return just before the hatching to relieve the males, who are seriously weakened from their ordeal.

Cracked Egg with Common Eider Hatchling

A bird's egg comprises a wondrous balance. It bears the weight of an incubating parent, and yet is not so thick that the grown hatchling cannot get out. When about to hatch, the eggs of Common Eiders benefit from the care and protection of their mother and other nonbreeding females that gather around the newborns and accompany the ducklings to the water. The downy hatchlings leave the nest within twenty-four hours and feed themselves as they learn to dive within one hour of entering the water.

European Cuckoo Baby

To hatch its young, the calculating female Cuckoo selects the nest of a suitable foster parent, which it momentarily frightens away before laying an egg whose color and size closely match those found within. The young Cuckoo often hatches before its nest-mates and instinctively ejects the other eggs from the nest. At three weeks of age, the Cuckoo baby weighs fifty times its birth weight. One of nature's most absurd tragicomedies unfolds as the diminutive adoptive parent feverishly collects food to satisfy a nestling more than twice its size!

Bewick's Wren with Nest in a Can

Bewick's Wrens usually build their nests in various cavities, usually natural crevices and abandoned Woodpecker holes, or in artificial structures such as this old tin can. The nest is a soft cup made with a foundation of twigs and bark, then lined with moss, leaves, hair, and feathers.

Birdhouses

While most birds prefer to build their own dwellings, nearly eighty-six North American species have been known to occupy artificial homes. However, like humans, birds place stringent requirements on potential homesites and will quickly vacate a birdhouse that is not "up to standard." The true test of a winning design is whether or not a bird will actually move in.

House Sparrow with Nest in Shorts Pocket

House Sparrows are not actually Sparrows at all but are a species of Old World Weaver Finches, a family noted for its ingenious nest-building ability. This little Sparrow found the pocket of my daughter's shorts left on a clothesline a suitable nesting hole, and constructed its nest with twigs and grass, then lined it with feathers, hair, string, and paper.

Satin Bowerbird Couple

Deep in the rainforests of Australia, the eccentric bright blue male Satin Bowerbird has an unusual yearly breeding ritual. He constructs an elaborate platform of grass strands and erects thin walls at both ends of this stage. He then decorates this "lover's lane" or bower, with a mishmash of odd trinkets and scraps. His only criterion: that these items be blue. Pleased with his architectural prowess, the male struts about his bower, proffering bits of blue at the arrival of an appreciative female.

Feathers

A single feather is composed of more than a million interlocking parts. Beak to tail, most birds are completely covered with them, whether with fluffy down or streamlined flight feathers. Not all birds fly or sing or build nests. Yet all birds share one feature: feathers. No bird lacks them or can survive without them. The plumage of some species, especially hawks and others that spend much of their lives on the wing, weighs more than their skeleton because their bones are so light.

Blue Tit Flock

The little Blue Tit is common to gardens and woodlands throughout Europe and western Asia. They travel in flocks and are natural gymnasts, adept at clinging to small branches at almost any angle. While they feed mostly on insects and seeds, these restless, inquisitive birds have been known to teach each other how to open traditional British foil-topped milk bottles, drinking the cream underneath. Flocks have even been observed following milkmen on morning deliveries in anticipation of their morning treat.

African Ostrich and Locust Finch

The Ostrich and Locust Finch are both native to Africa, but their habitats and physical characteristics couldn't be more different. The Ostrich is the largest living species of bird and flourishes in dry grasslands all over the world, but is one of the few birds that cannot fly. The brightly colored Locust Finch is a tiny bird, no more than 3½ inches in size. It prefers a moist habitat and moves in dense swarms in wet grasslands. It can be found only in parts of south and central Africa where there is sufficient water.

Peacock Feather

Darwin once said, "The eyespot of the Peacock's train feathers is probably the most beautiful object in the world." Peafowl are members of the Pheasant family and the three main species are native to Asia and Africa. The blue- or green-bodied Asian Peacocks are the most common in captivity. The males have resplendent iridescent train feathers that they spread in fan formation when courting the less colorful penhens.

Black Swans

Choose an elegant adjective and it has probably been used to describe the Swan. The long-necked, smooth-gliding Swan is the picturesque monarch of lakes and slow-moving rivers. Swans are among the most monogamous of birds, often faithful to the same mate year after year.

Vermillion Flycatchers

Vermillion Flycatchers are monogamous birds, choosing their mates after engaging in a complex ritual of nest selection. The male chooses potential nest sites, gives soliciting calls to nearby females to take a look at his selections, and flutters his wings in display when an interested female likes what she sees. After the pair construct their nest, the male feeds his mate insects every hour as she incubates the eggs. When the eggs hatch both parents feed their young by foraging for insects in flight as they sally back and forth from perch to prey.

Cracked Eggshells

Egg coloring is a phenomenon that defies simple explanation. The actual egg patterns, the distinctive blotches, streaks, spots, and scrawls, are the result of pigments absorbed by the porous "canvas" of the eggshell during its passage through the female's oviduct and are as individual as a human's fingerprint.

Songbirds in a Tree

(top to bottom: Red-eyed Vireo, Black-throated Green Warbler, Black-throated Blue Warbler, Western Tanager, Cape May Warbler, Song Sparrow) Bird songs are extremely complex, some consisting of up to eighty notes per second and up to four overlapping notes produced at once. Among those species that sing incessantly, the Red-eyed Vireo holds the avian record with over twenty-two thousand performances in a single day.

Loud, penetrating song is vital to the songbird's survival in the tangle of branches and leaves where visual displays are largely ineffective. Where songbirds choose to perform varies often according to their feeding niche—in this case the level in the tree canopy where they searh for insects. The Black-throated Blue Warbler consistently sings from limbs near the ground, a Black-throated Green Warbler from midway up, and the Cape May Warbler calls out from the treetops.

Bald Eagle Wing

The basic prerequisite of flight is the feathered wing. Light, strong, and flexible, the wing is an aerodynamic wonder, perfectly curved and stream-lined to slice the wind while gaining its support.

Greater Snow Goose

Native to the Arctic, Snow Geese begin their southward migration in fall in large flocks. As they travel from breeding to wintering grounds, they fly between 40 and 50 miles per hour and have been known to stay airborne as long as 70 hours and 1,700 miles. Their average flying altitude is about 3,000 feet, but they have been recorded at heights as high as 20,000 feet. These high-flying flocks can be identified by the undulating arcs they form as individuals at staggered heights rise and descend in imperfect V formation.

Young Great Crested Flycatcher

Born in nests often lined with discarded snake skins and plant material, hatchling Great Crested Flycatchers are tended to by both parents who feed them small insects and berries until they are ready to fend for themselves. The infants fledge fifteen to twenty days after hatching, when they are ready to fly. These migratory birds are native to the eastern United States, and migrate in winter to Florida and as far south as northern South America.

Long-tailed Tailorbird and Nest

The tiny Long-tailed Tailorbird fashions its astonishing nest out of living leaves using its fine pointed bill as a needle. The bird meticulously pierces an equal number of holes on each leaf edge and uses spider silk, cotton shreds, or fine grass as thread. Stitching back and forth through the holes, the bird joins the leaf seams together, tying knots as it sews and leaving an entrance hole on top. The female uses soft vegetable down, fine grass, and feathers to line the inside of the warm, safe cocoon, tailor-made for her eggs.

Kiwi

A native of New Zealand, the flightless Kiwi lacks most traditional bird attributes: It has exceedingly poor eyesight, no tail, and only the hint of wings. Its feathers look more like an old shaggy coat of ruffled brown hair than instruments conducive to flight. Regardless, the pear-shaped creature is well loved; it serves as New Zealand's national emblem. Pride in the Kiwi takes yet another form: New Zealanders commonly and affectionately refer to themselves as "kiwis."

Ring-billed Gull

The Ring-billed Gull is probably the most numerous Gull in North America and is an amazingly adaptable bird. It is equally at home at sea, near inland waterways and beaches, and in urban landscapes such as large grassy lawns and parking lots. Ring-billed Gulls are scavengers and will eat almost anything. They are able to snatch food from the water's surface while in flight.

Flamingo

Flamingos feed by poking their heads upside down into shallow water and trawling with their sieve-like bills. Their pink and red plumage is the colorful result of the adage "You are what you eat." The birds extract a natural dye from tiny crustaceans related to shrimp and from microscopic algae that tints their feathers.

Cinnamon Teal

Despite vast diversity, the 147 duck species can be divided into two simple categories: "divers," which plunge completely underwater for food, and "dabblers," which skim food from the water's surface or tip forward, tail pointed to the sky, to feed in the shallows. The Cinnamon Teal is a dabbler but it will also dive for food such as aquatic invertebrates and plants. When a predator is nearby, females will create a disturbance to draw attention away from the nests while the males tend to create a diversion by circling the area.

Scarlet Tanager Nest and Eggs

The Scarlet Tanager nest is composed of plant stems, grass, and rootlets. It is a coarsely woven, fairly shallow nest resembling beautifully constructed basketwork. The female builds the nest, gathering material mainly from the forest floor within her territory.

Birds' Eyes

(left to right, top to bottom: Wood Duck, Toucan, Flamingo, Great Horned Owl) The avian eye is a focal point of stunning beauty and color, but its superb capacity is equally remarkable. It performs its duties so successfully that three of the birds' other senses—taste, smell, and touch—are largely superfluous. The visual acuity of most species allows them to forage, avoid predators, and adjust for the rapid changes of aerial movement, all at once. Members of the Hawk family have eyesight that is estimated four to eight times sharper than human's.